DARTMOOR WALKS FOR MOTORISTS

Warne Gerrard Guides for Walkers

Walks for Motorists Series

CHESHIRE WALKS

CHILTERNS WALKS
    Northern
    Southern

COUNTY OF AVON WALKS

COUNTY DURHAM WALKS

COTSWOLD WALKS
    Northern
    Southern

DARTMOOR WALKS

EXMOOR WALKS

JERSEY WALKS

LAKE DISTRICT WALKS
    Central
    Northern
    Western

LONDON COUNTRYSIDE WALKS
    North West
    North East
    South West
    South East

GREEN LONDON WALKS
    (both circular and cross country)

LOTHIAN AND SOUTH EAST BORDERS WALKS

MIDLAND WALKS

NORTH YORK MOORS WALKS
    North and East
    West and South

PEAK DISTRICT WALKS

PENDLESIDE AND BRONTE COUNTRY WALKS

SNOWDONIA WALKS
    Northern

SOUTH DEVON WALKS

SOUTH DOWNS WALKS

WYE VALLEY WALKS

YORKSHIRE DALES WALKS

FURTHER DALES WALKS

Long Distance and Cross Country Walks

WALKING THE PENNINE WAY

RAMBLES IN THE DALES

Contents

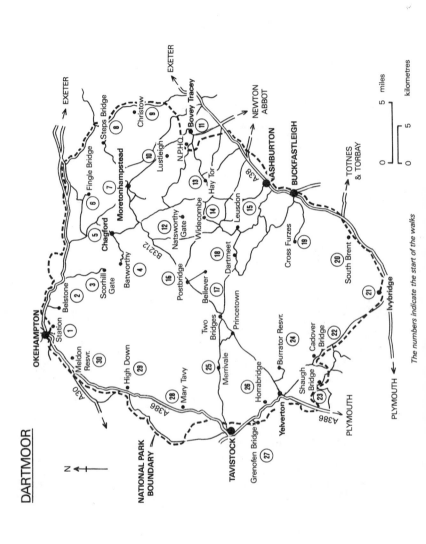

DARTMOOR

The numbers indicate the start of the walks

Introduction

It is not my intention in these introductory pages to give a history or description of Dartmoor. There are plenty of books available which provide that sort of information. However, certain features which may be new to the reader are mentioned in the walk descriptions, and it seems preferable to deal with them here rather than to define, say, the ruins of a prehistoric hut in perhaps five separate places in the book.

I also feel that the public concept of National Parks is so hazy that a few words on that aspect are required, particularly in relation to public access.

Lastly, although the form of the walk descriptions could hardly be more simple, some advice on their layout and the conventions used will help the reader derive most enjoyment from them.

The elements of Dartmoor which are particularly its own are the granite rock and the prehistoric remains. To these must be added the feeling of freedom induced by the atmosphere of wilderness on the open moor when all traces of modern civilisation are left behind.

This concept of wilderness can sometimes be heightened by the ruined relics of prehistoric man, through a sense of desertion and abandonment, and nowhere else in Britain can you find these remains so thickly grouped. In places, and Merrivale (Walk 25) is one, the low walls of his huts are clustered together among the natural boulders of the moor so that the casual stranger may not recognise them for what they are. It is the enduring quality of the rock and the lack of any large scale subsequent disturbance which has allowed so many antiquities to be preserved.

The granite manifests itself to the visitor most prominently in the tors, a name derived from the same root which has given us the word 'tower'. Often they are hilltop excrescences, but they come in numerous shapes and situations, and are sometimes found as hillside crags and outcrops. Some of them are not granite, for where the metamorphic rock is exposed on the fringes of the moor, tors occur of that border stone. Leigh Tor (Walk 15) and the Sourton Tors (Walk 30) are examples.

I have lost count of the times I have arrived at Combestone Tor (Walk 18) with a party of strangers to the moor and been asked 'Is it man-made?' Having replied that it is natural, the next question 'How are tors formed then?' is asked more easily than it is answered; even the experts cannot agree! But some facts are conceded by everyone.

Granite is an igneous rock, that is it was formed by the cooling of an upthrust of molten magma from within the earth. The magma was forced up against an overlay of rocks which have since been completely eroded by the natural elements: wind, rain and frost, over something like 295,000,000 years.

Not only has the overlay been totally denuded, but the granite has itself been broken and shattered by the extremes of climate over millions of years. This has caused the litter of rocks – the name clitter which is given to them is particularly apt – on so many slopes below the tors.

One theory suggests that before the rocks were exposed they were subjected to the chemical action of water circulating through the joints and weaknesses of the blocks.

Another theory is more straightforward, and supposes that the tors are the remnants of the hilltop when all around has been fractured and eroded. The Dartmoor National Park Authority publishes a leaflet called the *Outline of the Geology* but it skates round the ticklish problem of the origin of the tors.

On the tor summits will often be found round hollows, rock basins they are called, of such regular shape as to suggest a human origin. (In fact, even between the wars the Ordnance Survey were showing rock basins on their maps in a Gothic typeface.) However, they are entirely natural, and owe their formation to the action of climatic forces on the crystalline character of the granite. The process probably begins with a large felspar crystal breaking up and leaving a hole which gets larger as the wind blows the granules round and round. Frost, ice, rain, wind and millions of years do the rest.

Prehistoric remains dating from the Bronze Age, say from 2500 BC to 750 BC, are especially plentiful on Dartmoor, but too much reliance should not be put on exact dates. They can best be divided into settlement and ritual sites.

The settlement sites most commonly found are the ruined stone walls of the circular huts – they are called hut circles on Ordnance Survey maps. The earliest date from about 2000 BC and overlap into the Iron Age, some being occupied up to about 50 BC. Mostly they occur in groups, and may be enclosed within a wall as at Grimspound (Walk 12). The huts had pointed conical roofs of some sort of thatch supported on wooden rafters. A gap in the wall for the door on the south side can sometimes be seen. Over 2000 huts have been identified, but many have been destroyed by later wall builders and field clearers. Any attempt to guess a prehistoric population is bound to fail. We do not know if the tribes or family groups were settled or nomadic, but towards the end of the period they became less pastoral and more inclined to cultivate crops. They were peaceful people.

In recent years an extensive web of field or territorial boundaries has been discovered and plotted. They take the form of earth and stone banks and are called reaves on Dartmoor. You will see one of the best of these patterns from Combestone Tor (Walk 18) which has taken the deep valley of the Dart in its stride. Another field system can be seen on the slopes of Kes Tor (Walks 3 and 4).

Iron Age hillforts with earthworks suggest tribal warfare and a breaking down of the former peaceful way of life. There are examples round the fringe of the moor at Cranbrook Castle and the Dewerstone (Walks 7 and 23).

The ritual sites can be subdivided into burial and worship sites. Barrows and cairns are common and are heaps of earth (barrows) or stone (cairns) over a burial. Sometimes the barrow has been worn or dug away, leaving only the burial chambers, a stone-sided receptacle looking like a large matchbox. The stone lid has usually been displaced. These are cists, kists or kistvaens.

Associated with these kinds of burials are the mysterious stone rows. These are single, double or triple lines of stones set on end, running in roughly straight lines over various distances. These can vary between the length of a cricket pitch, and the longest stone row in the world in the Erme valley – over two miles. No-one knows what they were erected for. As processional ways to the burial of a chief, perhaps? (See Walks 4 and 25).

Menhirs or standing stones are often found with stone rows. (See Walks 4 and 25). Lastly there are the worship sites, circles of standing stones which may have been some sort of temple – a kind of mini-Stonehenge. (See Walks 3 and 25).

No evidence has come to light to show that prehistoric man cut or shaped the stones he used in his buildings or monuments. He simply used the material lying about on the surface – moorstone it is usually called. With better tools and greater skill his sucessors have used the native rock to good effect to produce a wealth of interest from this intractable stone, and many artifacts will be noticed in the various walks. Besides stone buildings, look out for clapper bridges, direction posts, stiles, crosses, troughs, slotted gateposts, mould stones and edge-runners. An edge-runner is a large stone wheel which was walked round a massive stone trough by a horse to crush apples for cider, to grind bark for the tanneries and to crush young green gorse for animal feed. Gorse is rich in minerals. The walls of Dartmoor are worth a close study; some are ramshackle affairs which threaten to fall down if you as much as touch them, but somehow manage to stay up, while others are more robust and a pleasure to look at. Fortunately there are still men on the moor capable of building a good wall.

If you want to know more about these features you cannot do better than buy *The Archaeology of Dartmoor* which is written by a professional archaeologist with a feel for his subject. It is published by the Dartmoor National Park Authority. You will find the chronological chart of the different types of site very useful.

The cheap booklets I have mentioned in this introduction are two of the publications provided by the National Park Authority as part of its interpretive service. Dartmoor was created one of the ten British National Parks in 1951, a designation which in England and Wales is a planning term, placing these areas at the top of the landscape hierarchy.

A committee of Devon County Council has the statutory duty to preserve and enhance the natural beauty of the Park and to promote its enjoyment by the public. At the same time the committee has to have regard to the needs of agriculture and forestry, and must concern itself with the social and economic well-being of the inhabitants of the Park. The National Park Authority is therefore the planning committee for the area.

In Britain, unlike the USA, all National Park land is in private ownership. The term National Park can be misleading. It is not 'nationalised' or a 'park' in the accepted sense. Hundreds of small landowners, the Water Authority, the Forestry Commission, the National Trust and the Duchy of Cornwall all have a stake in the Park. So what about the open moorland? It must belong to someone.

Yes, it does, to dozens of different owners, and much of it is common land, which is an ancient term to describe land owned by one person over which others have certain rights. These rights are usually to graze animals, to dig peat for fuel, to take heather for thatching and stone and sand to repair houses. They only go with certain properties on the moor and do not entitle anyone to take what he likes. It is only common land to the commoners. There is no public right of access to most of the common land of Dartmoor (except for certain well-defined areas), although this may be rectified.

The day I write this (late July 1979) I read in *The Western Morning News* that the House of Lords Select Committee has accepted the Dartmoor Commons Bill which was debated in an eleven-day hearing in June. The Bill, jointly promoted by Devon County Council (on behalf of the Dartmoor National Park Committee) and the Dartmoor Commoners' Association, seeks to give a legal right of access on foot to the public over the Dartmoor commons, and at the same time allow the commoners to manage the commons for the purpose of livestock husbandry.

The position hitherto has been that on much of the open moor a *de facto*, assumed, traditional or customary 'right' of access has been allowed, but this isn't the same as a *de jure* or legal right.

However, public rights of way which may be footpaths or bridleways cross the moor and thread their way through the enclosed country. These are maintained by the National Park rangers (they used to be called wardens) with voluntary labour to assist them. They erect signposts, build stiles, clear fallen trees and apply orange waymark blobs to gateposts and tree trunks to help the walker.

Other ways the National Park Authority helps the public are

through the provision of information centres, a programme of guided walks and the special Dartmoor bus services. Information can be obtained from: The Information Officer, Dartmoor National Park Authority, Parke, Haytor Road, Bovey Tracey, Devon, TQ13 9JQ; Bovey Tracey 832093.

Dartmoor is no museum. Farming, both lowland and hill-farming, is carried on in the traditional way, and in certain places like Ashburton, Buckfastleigh and Moretonhampstead there are small industries. It is a dynamic place, with things changing all the time, despite the feeling of communion with former ages which is so strong.

These changes, as I have already indicated, can affect you, the visitor, if the Dartmoor Commons Bill becomes law – to your advantage. But footpaths also change. Here and there over the years the route of paths may be improved, so be ready for the occasional difficulty. Usually these will be well signposted so as to get the walker round the problem. However, signposts get knocked down by animals, yellow houses are painted pink and trees used as landmarks are sawn down. If in doubt and provided there is someone nearby – ask. Better this than to trespass.

Dartmoor is roughly round, so the 30 walks in this book are taken in clockwise order starting from Okehampton. They all start from places where cars can be parked. You should read each walk description first for maximum enjoyment. Otherwise how would you know that a torch is useful, though not necessary, for Walks 3 and 4?

The usual descriptive convention has been followed for river banks. The left bank and right bank are always the left bank and right bank looking downstream.

Each walk description has the 1:50,000 OS sheet number noted at the top. In fact, the OS 1in tourist map covers the whole moor, but the details show up less clearly than on the metric map. The sketch maps, which are not strictly to scale, should be adequate for finding your way on the walk, but OS maps will tell you what is to be seen on either side which the sketch maps will not.

What else should you have with you? This will clearly depend on the time of the year, the weather and the length of the walk, but wear comfortable clothes and especially sensible footwear. Boots are best, but it's quite possible to do Walks 14 and 24 in shoes. A waterproof is advisable. Whether you take food and drink will depend on the time you intend to take over the walk, and the availability of refreshments en route. Where this is possible it is stated in the walk description.

Certain walks have a warning that you should be accomplished in map and compass work if you intend to follow them in misty conditions. This is no conventional warning, but heart-felt advice not to get yourself into a dangerous situation. If the worst happens, and a member of the group is lost or injured, someone should get to a telephone, dial 999 and ask for the police. There is a Dartmoor

Rescue Group, and they are called out by the police. If you are on your own when something goes wrong, let us hope that someone knows where you are! It is a good idea to leave a message before setting out.

Parts of the northern moor are used by the Army as a gunnery range. None of the walks in this book enter this area, but if necessary you can get details of the firing programme from Dartmoor National Park information centres, post offices, police stations and hotels in the Dartmoor area, or by telephoning Exeter 70164 or Plymouth 701924.

These cautionary words are not meant to deter you from setting off, but to ensure that you are ready for the worst that Dartmoor can throw at you. Properly prepared you will enjoy your walks to the full. And may I ask please that you observe the Country Code?

Keep dogs under proper control.
Guard against fire risk.
Keep to the paths across farmland.
Fasten all gates.
Go carefully on country roads.
Leave no litter.
Respect the life of the countryside.
Safeguard water supplies.
Avoid damaging fences, hedges and walls.
Protect wildlife, wild plants and trees.

Walk 1   The East Okement Valley

3½ miles (5.5km)

OS sheet 191

Half this walk from the edge of Okehampton is in the wooded East
Okement valley, and there are a couple of places which involve a
minor scramble and a steep climb.

Leave your car outside the disused Okehampton station, which is
on the higher side of the town. Turn up George Street opposite the
town hall and then into Station Road which leads to the station.

Okehampton is tucked away under the northern slopes of
Dartmoor, and as it straddles the East and West Okement valleys
there is a choice of approach to the moor. The town has some good
stores, including an excellent bookshop and a walking equipment
shop.

From the station yard pass through a small green gate opposite the
old station buildings and go down the stone steps to a level track at
the bottom. This is the route of a long-disused mineral tramway.
Turn right and follow it for ¾ mile, looping left near the East
Okement river and then right to pass beneath Fatherford viaduct,
the railway approach to Okehampton from Exeter.

Here the path runs into beautiful woodland and carries on up-
river on the west bank. The path crosses the Moor Brook by a
footbridge 800yd from the viaduct and continues up the main river
past a series of cataracts. The path gets steep and hands may be
necessary to steady the person. After the roughest section the path
levels out and drops to Chapel Ford 700yd from the Moor Brook.
Here there is a footbridge across the East Okement as well as
stepping stones and a ford. Wild mink are sometimes seen at this
spot. (Walk 2 passes here).

Now retrace your steps for 150yd to a path junction on the slope,
and take the higher path, instead of the valley path you came along.
This is a steep climb through woods, but is fairly short. When the
path reaches a wall at the top and leaves the woods, follow the path
round to the west, contouring the hillside, with large gorse bushes to
the right. Stop to admire the view across the well-wooded Moor
Brook valley to Ashbury Tor on the facing hilltop.

Now make for the wall corner ahead, bear left and up a lane
leading to an open space just outside Lower Halstock farm. Pass
through the gate and the farmyard and take the farm road to the top
of Camp Hill.

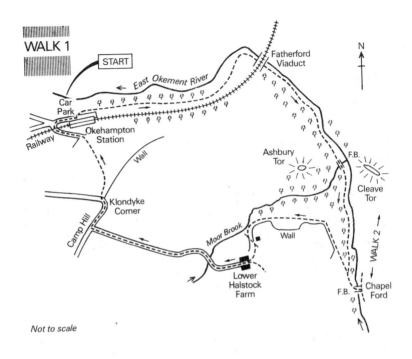

WALK 1

START

East Okement River

Fatherford
Viaduct

N

Car
Park

Railway

Okehampton
Station

Wall

Ashbury
Tor

F.B.

Cleave
Tor

Klondyke
Corner

Camp Hill

Moor Brook

Wall

WALK 2

Lower
Halstock
Farm

F.B.

Chapel
Ford

Not to scale

Along here you will see Okehampton camp over to your left. The Army began to use Dartmoor for training in the 1870s, and are firmly entrenched on the northern moor, where they fire live ammunition, explode demolition charges, fly helicopters and engage in many kinds of less destructive training. The boundaries of the firing areas are marked by 6ft red and white poles and walkers must on no account enter a firing area when live ammunition is being used. At these times red flags are flown from flagpoles in the vicinity.

Turn right when you reach Camp Hill, admire the view to the north-west and go down as far as the hairpin bend, Klondyke Corner. Now enter the lower of two gates and follow the well-defined path to the bottom exit of this field. This path is much used for tobogganing after snow. From the gate follow the track down under the railway to the station yard.

Walk 2   Chapel Ford and the Belstone Tors
4 miles (6.5km)

OS sheet 191

This is an exhilarating walk along a rocky hilltop after visiting the East Okement valley. Not much fun in mist; you won't see anything!

To get to the start of the walk at Belstone, turn south from the A30 at Tongue End, two miles east of Okehampton. Belstone is one mile away. Cars may be parked in the village, but the best place is opposite the village hall.

Belstone stands high between the rivers Taw and East Okement, and is built round two village greens, on one of which stands the village stocks.

Leave Belstone by a road at the top of the village signposted 'Okehampton indirect'. Follow it for half a mile to the lane on the left just past Cleave House (Dartmoor Riding Centre). Turn in here. There is a muddy stretch, but one is soon through it and out of a gate on to a stretch of smooth turf. Leave the track and walk straight ahead to Cleave Tor, or the Coronet of Rocks as it is sometimes called. Cleave Tor is not a granite tor, but is of metamorphic rock, which is found round the edge of the moor.

Now return to the track and follow it along the hillside. Just past an iron seat against the wall the track forks. Take the lower option which leads down to Chapel Ford (visited from the other direction in Walk 1) where there is a footbridge, stepping stones and a ford. Continue upstream with the East Okement river on your right, pass through a hedge gap and start to climb the hill on a path in line with the distant tor summits, your ultimate destination.

The present path merges with a track coming up from the left and soon crosses the major track from Belstone (left) to Cullever Steps (right). 80yd beyond this track turn right along a lesser, but nonetheless ancient track which was made by the peat cutters bringing back fuel to their homes from the high moor.

The aiming point is now Winter Tor on the hillside ⅔ mile ahead and due south, and the track leads to its higher side. Carry on up to the top of the ridge, and on the watershed turn left and walk up the spine of this feature past Higher Tor to the crest of the ridge where the several summits of the Belstone Tors prod the sky. To the east is the great bowl of Taw Plain (Taw Marsh on the maps) and beyond the massive border height of Cosdon Beacon (Cawsand Beacon on the maps; the Ordnance Survey's interpretation of Dartmoor place-names is not good!).

15

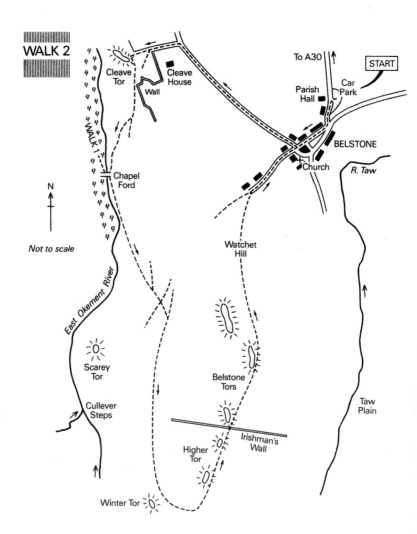

WALK 2

Cleave
Tor

Cleave
House

Wall

To A30

Parish
Hall

Car
Park

START

BELSTONE

Church

R. Taw

WALK 1

Chapel
Ford

N

Not to scale

East Okement River

Watchet
Hill

Scarey
Tor

Cullever
Steps

Belstone
Tors

Taw
Plain

Irishman's
Wall

Higher
Tor

Winter Tor

Continue along here, picking your way through the boulders. Passing over this ridge and taking a general east–west course you will see the tumbled ruins of a wall. This is known as Irishman's Wall, after a citizen of that country who had acquisitive designs on part of the moor hereabouts and sought to enclose it. He employed a gang of his fellows who built a considerable length of wall. The local inhabitants stood back but when the project was far advanced they met in strength and threw portions of the wall over, rendering it useless. The Irishman gave up and left the neighbourhood.

Eventually you drop down the north slope to Watchet Hill across which numerous old stonecutters' tracks lead to Belstone. A hundred years ago Belstone granite was much used for building, gateposts, feeding troughs and so on. The stone was roughly cut on the moor where it lay, and finished off in Belstone where life was carried on to the ring of iron on stone.

The road is met at Watchet Hill Gate, and a steep drop down leads quickly back to the village.

Walk 3   Gidleigh Common and Gidleigh

4 miles (6.5km)

OS sheet 191

This is a pleasant varied walk with some climbing towards the end. There is a stretch of open moor at the beginning, so take care in mist.

Park your car at the small car park at Scorhill Gate on the moor edge above Gidleigh, north-east Dartmoor. This is best reached by driving south 3½ miles along the margin of the moor from Ramsley Corner on the A30 at South Zeal, and keeping right at every fork except the first 'No Through Road' sign.

From the car park walk up the funnel of open land between walls aiming for the top left corner. Here follow the track over the hilltop ahead and slightly left. Pause on the summit to take in the view if clear.

Exmoor is in the far distance behind; Cosdon is the large round hill with a heathery crown; Steeperton Tor is the hill with a prominent hut; Wild Tor spreads itself along the skyline, as does Watern Tor which is slightly closer; Hangingstone Hill is behind Watern Tor and betrays its presence with a flagpole. Kes Tor is the large lump one mile to the south with the remains of Iron Age fields on its slopes.

Halfway down the far side of Scorhill look out for the standing stones of Scorhill Circle 250yd away from the track right. Walk across to it. This is a Bronze Age monument, probably 4000 years old and presumably it had some religious significance. See how some of the stones have been damaged at the hands of latterday drillers, and others were carried or dragged 30yd downhill to reinforce the nearby leat bank.

Now head directly to the foot of the Batworthy enclosure wall crossing the leat en route. In the bed of the North Teign river here is an enormous boulder with a natural hole worn through it. This is the tolmen. It has been shifted by a flood since lying in the position where it was worn through.

Walk upstream to a single-span clapper bridge over the Walla Brook, then back towards the wall to cross the North Teign by Teign clapper. The two rivers were deepened and walled up by the medieval tin streamers to lower the water-table up-river, so as to make it easier to work the valley gravels. From here follow the Batworthy wall for ⅔ mile making your own route to avoid some wet

18

WALK 3

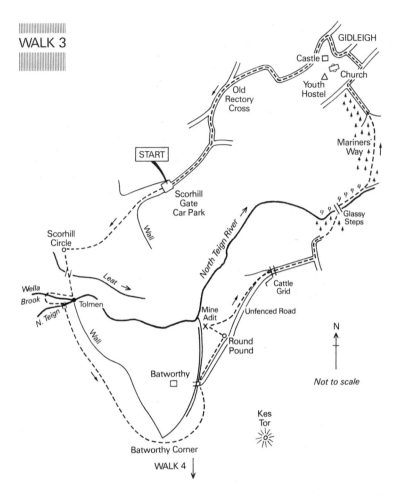

patches, then turn the corner left and join the road at a small parking place. (Walk 4 starts from here.)

Follow the road to the Round Pound which has three thorn trees growing from it, and causes the road to kink. This is a 2000-year-old hut, or rather the ruins of one, standing within an enclosure. It would have had a conical roof with some sort of thatching. Downhill from here in about 100yd is a tin mine adit dating from 100 years ago. Water trickles out, but the tunnel is fairly short and the roof seems safe enough for a brief exploration. You may get your feet wet. A torch is useful.

Return to the road and follow it over the cattle grid and downhill to the first bend. Turn left here through a gate and follow the

19

waymarks into the forest and down to the footbridge at Glassy Steps. Here one is on the so-called Mariners' Way, which may be folklore, but suggests that this was the cross-Devon foot link between the thriving ports of Dartmouth and Bideford in medieval times.

Carry on along the left bank of the North Teign for perhaps 300yd and turn up left by a signpost. After a steep climb the path levels out, leaves the plantation by a gate and soon reaches a road.

Turn right here, and left at the next turning by a large tree and phone box. This is Gidleigh – hardly a village, rather the centre of a scattered parish, but possessing a Youth Hostel, a lovely church, a late Norman castle and a pound (for animal strays). Jackdaws clatter round the castle ruins, rooks croak from their trees behind, and the whole atmosphere has a timelessness it is hard to discover elsewhere.

At the junction just past the pound (right) turn up steeply left, and the hill soon levels out into a delightful lane. Look out for slotted gateposts along this lane, particularly on the left after the second sharp corner. Field security relied on separate poles wedged in the grooves rather than a hinged gate. They are probably about 200 years old.

Bear left at Old Rectory Cross, keep left at the 'No Through Road' sign and right at the T-junction, and this brings one back to the car park.

Walk 4

4 miles (6.5km)

Chagford Common and the Mariners' Way

OS sheet 191

This is a varied walk among prehistoric antiquities, border tors and along old tracks. There is one wet section on the way back. The walk should not be attempted in mist unless you are accomplished with a map and compass.

The walk starts from the small car park at Batworthy-on-the-Moor. This is reached from Chagford by following the signs reading 'Kes Tor Rock'. Chagford itself is 1½ miles west of the A382 between Moretonhampstead and the A30.

From the small car park climb the steep bank to get your bearings, then follow the wall uphill, taking care not to be too close to it as there is an unpleasant mire from which the little stream springs.

At the corner of the wall make for an irregular line of stones to the south. This is a prehistoric stone row, a linear monument associated with a burial, as a disturbed interment site will be found at the top end of the row. Another row meets it at an angle, a third carries on over the hill, and a fourth may be found over the ridge heading towards the Longstone, a 10ft-high standing stone which is in fact on the line of a row, and not a terminal point. These remains and the related cairns are not more recent than about 1400 BC. The letters incised on the Longstone stand for Gidleigh parish and Duchy of Cornwall. The Duke of Cornwall (the Prince of Wales as it happens) owns a good deal of Lydford parish and the Longstone is a parish boundary stone for Lydford and Gidleigh parishes, and for Chagford too.

Now turn round and head for Kes Tor across flat moorland. Climb to the top – the east side has an easy route up – and take in the view. You are 1432ft above sea level. The large rock pool up here is one of Dartmoor's biggest rock basins, a natural feature caused by weathering. Frequently it is filled with rocks, but I have seen it empty of debris and containing 2ft of water. Small basins will be seen elsewhere on the top, in various stages of growth.

Now head slightly east of south across the moor to Middle Tor and on in the same direction to Frenchbeer Tor. These two tors have nothing special to show. At Frenchbeer Tor, turn east to where the nearby wall goes down to the road. Two hut circles will be passed on the way.

At the cattle grid turn left and go downhill to the hamlet of

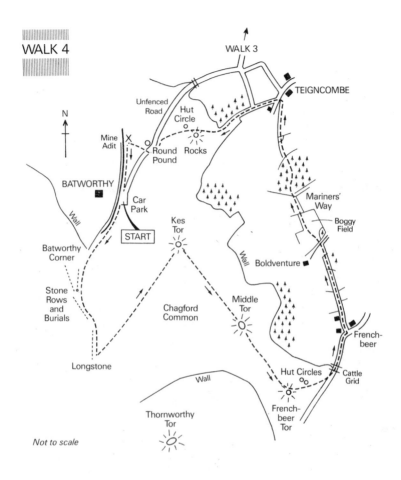

WALK 3

N

Unfenced
Road

Hut
Circle

TEIGNCOMBE

Mine
Adit

Round
Pound

Rocks

BATWORTHY

Car
Park

Mariners'
Way

Boggy
Field

START

Kes
Tor

Batworthy
Corner

Wall

Boldventure

Stone
Rows
and
Burials

Chagford
Common

Middle
Tor

Wall

French-
beer

Longstone

Wall

Hut Circles

Cattle
Grid

French-
beer

Thornworthy
Tor

French-
beer
Tor

Not to scale

Frenchbeer. At the footpath signpost turn left and follow the Mariners' Way to Teigncombe. As mentioned in Walk 3, this is possibly folklore, but a foot route across Devon from Dartmouth to Bideford has been postulated, and where it touches eastern Dartmoor it is reasonably well authenticated. This section is well maintained and waymarked by the National Park Authority.

The path follows a gated hillside track which enters Boldventure farm meadow by a stile after 400yd and leaves it opposite entering a particularly wet and boggy field by another stile. The way is clear across the spongy turf; the efforts of previous walkers have ensured that. Leave this field (with relief!) by a gate in the far corner and head for another gate across a flat field.

The next stretch is through a plantation, at the end of which a ladder stile gets you back into a field. From here make for a stile hidden in a clump of trees ahead, and then follow a ditch-type stream to a pair of gates which bring you out into the lane at the hamlet of Teigncombe. Here, it is said, there used to be a resthouse on the Mariners' Way.

Turn up the lane left as indicated by the signpost. It is a rough, rocky lane; almost like a dried-up watercourse. Its name is Teigncombe Common Lane. Carry straight on at a turning right, and pass out onto the open moor at a hunting gate.

Make for the top right corner of this narrowing funnel of walls – it's called a stroll on Dartmoor – and bear half right to pass beside an un-named isolated cluster of rocks, and down to the road. You will pass a hut circle on the way.

At the road look out for the Round Pound, which has three thorn trees growing from it, and whose ruined foundations have caused the road to hiccup off course. Standing within this enclosure is the ruin of a 2000-year-old circular hut, perhaps the chief's house among this scattered settlement on the slopes of Kes Tor whose broken-down fieldbanks are all around you. Down the slope from here in 100yd is a mine adit, a tunnel going into the hillside for 20yd or so and well worth seeing. Water trickles from its portal, but the roof appears to be sound enough to permit a brief exploration. A torch is a good idea. This was probably a tin mine about 100 years ago. A ruined building stands by the entrance.

From here follow the stream back to the car park.

Walk 5
3 miles (4.8km)

Chagford and the Banks of the River Teign

OS sheet 191

This is an easy field-path and minor road walk taking in the environs of Chagford.

Chagford is 1½ miles west of the A382 between Moretonhampstead and the A30. A large car park is signposted from the Square.

Chagford is a delightful Dartmoor border town the inhabitants of which have been aware of its attraction as an inland holiday resort for about 100 years. There are many hotels and guest houses in the immediate area, and the shops are surprisingly good for a small town. The popularity of Chagford with visitors is not surprising, bearing in mind the rich and varied scenery near at hand, and the places of historic interest awaiting discovery. In medieval times it was a stannary town (stannum: tin); one of the four Dartmoor towns to which tin was brought for valuation and for the paying of coinage dues. The buildings of Chagford make a harmonious group, with the church and the Three Crowns Hotel outstanding.

From the car park, walk past the Three Crowns Hotel, across the Square and down Mill Street, forking right at the Moorlands Hotel, a nineteenth-century wool warehouse conversion. At the crossroads at the bottom of the hill turn right past the kennels of the Mid-Devon Hunt, cross Chagford Bridge and turn in at the signposted gate just beyond. From here the path is well defined and easily followed as it is a popular local walk. It traces the river downstream without always being actually on the bank. The large building on the opposite bank was built as a woollen mill. Wool was Chagford's trade after the slump in Dartmoor tin about 1700.

After ¾ mile, as you cross a footbridge over Rushford Mill leat, the next stage is not immediately obvious. As you leave the bridge, a stile, at first invisible, is in the hedge 100yd ahead. Cross here and make for the next stile at the near end of Rushford Bridge across the field. Chagford swimming pool is 200yd along the road to the left. It is open in the summer and makes use of the disused Rushford Mill pond.

Cross Rushford Bridge and climb the stile on the south side, following a fence round to a stile at the far end of the field which gets one out onto the main approach road to Chagford. Turn left here and right at Broomhill after 50yd, turning up a narrow path after 50yd which leads to a stile. Cross this, enter the field and head half

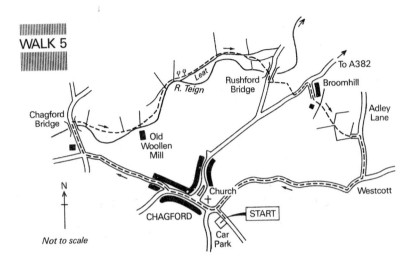

To A382

Broomhill

Adley
Lane

Rushford
Bridge

Leat

R. Teign

Chagford
Bridge

Old
Woollen
Mill

Church

Westcott

N

CHAGFORD

START

Not to scale

Car
Park

right for a stile out of sight in a dip using a white slate-roofed house
as a direction point.

From the stile in the dip head for a tiled bungalow and this gets
one out into a short track leading to Adley Lane. Turn right here,
right again at the hamlet of Westcott, and Chagford is reached after
a steep end-of-walk uphill pull.

Walk 6   Fingle Bridge and the Teign Gorge
4 miles (6.5km)

OS sheet 191

This is a beautiful walk with a climb at the beginning and later some roughish walking along the banks of the river Teign. There is also an opportunity to visit a twentieth-century castle – Castle Drogo (National Trust).

Park your car at Fingle Bridge, which is tucked away on the river Teign in north-east Dartmoor, one mile from Drewsteignton, which is itself signposted from the A382 and A30. There are public lavatories.

Fingle Bridge dates from about 1570 and has withstood enormous floods in those 400 years. The road up through the woods to the south is not recommended for ordinary cars.

From the Anglers' Rest, walk along the road for 200yd away from the bridge, and turn up a path left which climbs steeply through woods. Look out for the bulky nests of wood ants.

Where the path leaves the woods it levels out and fine views of northern Dartmoor open up, with the square snout of Castle Drogo sticking out one mile ahead. Gorse now verges the path, known as the Hunters' Path.

The craggy twin buttresses of Sharp Tor – one of ten of this name on Dartmoor – are reached. This tor is of metamorphic rock, not granite, and anyone without a head for heights should stay away from the edge. From here it is possible to turn off the Hunters' Path and visit Castle Drogo, provided it is open, and rejoin the path at Hunts Tor, on the spur below the castle.

If you wish to do this, walk up the path away from the tor and follow a grassy glade through the gorse; the drive leading to the castle is reached in about 400yd. Turn left here, walk to the car park and pay your admission at the shop, unless you are a National Trust member.

The building is worth a visit, as it is the last great country house that will ever be built in England, and a granite tour de force. It was constructed between 1910 and 1930 by Julius Drewe and the architect was Sir Edwin Lutyens. Of course it is a castle in name only. Teas are available, and there is a beautiful formal garden as well as acres of land around the castle.

The Hunters' Path continues on a slightly downhill course (for those who have not diverted to the castle) and reaches the spur of

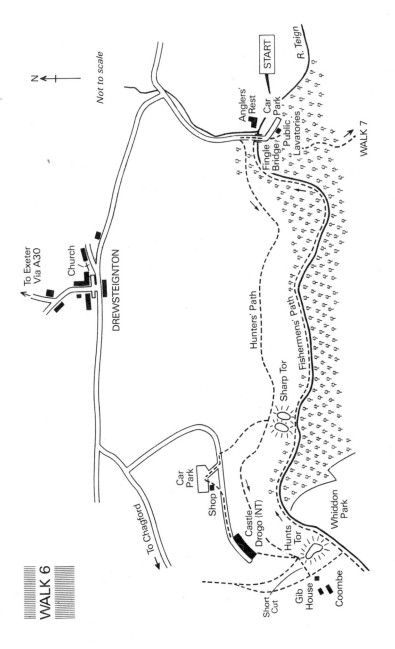

WALK 6

N

Not to scale

To Exeter
Via A30

Church

DREWSTEIGNTON

To Chagford

Car
Park

Shop

Castle
Drogo (NT)

Short
Cut

Gib
House

Hunts
Tor

Coombe

Whiddon
Park

Hunters' Path

Fishermens' Path

Sharp Tor

Anglers'
Rest

Fingle
Bridge

Car
Park

Public
Lavatories

START

R. Teign

WALK 7

Hunts Tor which marks the western end of the Teign Gorge. From here look across at the facing hillside, Whiddon Park. The massive wall around it, well over 6ft high, was meant to keep deer within its bounds.

On Hunts Tor walk steeply down a path through the bracken on a line with the thatched farm – Coombe. This brings one down to Gibhouse, another attractive thatched building in this pleasant backwater. (A more gentle descent to the same place involves walking away from the river for about 400yd, then coming back to the Teign along the lower path.) Turn left and follow the good path to the river Teign, noting how the owner of Gibhouse guards his vegetables against the deer with a 6ft fence.

Turn left at the river and follow this riverside path, the Fisherman's Path, back to Fingle Bridge, a distance of two miles. The walk is level but here and there tree roots provide minor obstacles. In several places the rock has fragmented to form scree slopes on the left, a feature not often met with on Dartmoor.

As you near the end of the walk, look out for an inscribed boulder in the river 50yd upstream from Fingle Bridge, bearing the words 'W.Brely 1884'. He was the miller at Fingle Mill, now ruinous, but still to be seen as a few dwarf walls 300yd below the bridge on the right bank. A fire destroyed the mill in 1894.

Walk 7   Moretonhampstead to Cranbrook Castle

5 or 7 miles (8 or 11km)

OS sheet 191

This is a field-path and minor road walk with a remarkable number of stiles – 23 I think. There is one stiff hill at the beginning.

Moretonhampstead is a busy little town astride the B3212 and A382. The unusual colonnaded almshouses (1637) in Cross Street are worth seeing. Leave your car in either of the two public car parks.

Leave Moretonhampstead by the Chagford road (Ford Street). At the end of the built-up area, at the top of a small hill, turn right at a road signposted to Howton and Uppacott and after 50yd take the Butterdon fork.

Climb steadily, and after 500yd, nearly at the top of a steep section, climb a stone stile to the left (signposted) and walk diagonally across the field to a stile in the far top corner. Follow the next field edge to a third stile, and carry on beside the hedge to the fourth stile. From here the line of the path is visible ahead across a shallow valley following the hedge banks. This is a surprisingly direct cross-country route.

The next stile admits the walker to a plantation with a low row of stones picking out the path a few feet from the hedge. At the next field boundary a minor road is crossed and the path continues beyond, again beside a plantation with the dwarf wall still present. Now leave the trees and enter a field, still with the hedge to the left, and beyond the next stile you have to cross a wet 20yd section where a small stream has to be negotiated by a mixture of stepping stones, causeway and clapper bridge. An enormous stone slab stile admits one to a field, followed by two more, then a patch of open moor – Butterdon – is reached.

The same general direction is followed for 300yd, when a solitary monolith (unmapped) is passed. The next stile is 100yd past the standing stone and admits the walker to a field. At the bottom of this field pass through a muddy open gateway and continue on the same hedge line, heading for Cranbrook farm visible ahead. Exit to the road by a ladder stile beside the field gate and turn left.

Follow this quiet road for 400yd to a triangular road junction where there is an ancient stone direction post in the south-west corner. Turn right here, and after 100yd go left up a signposted path to Cranbrook Castle, an Iron Age hill camp with the remains of

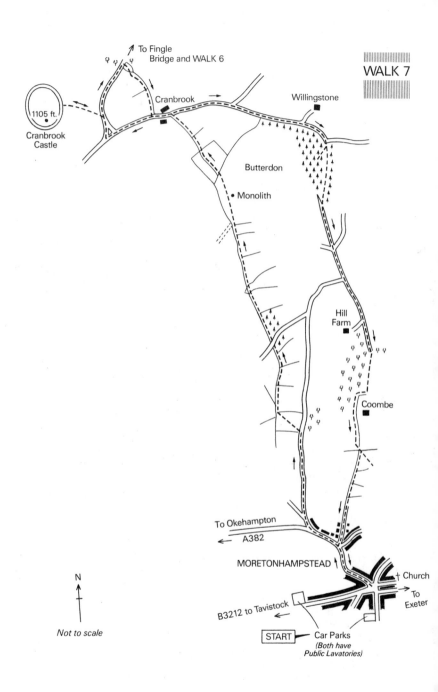

To Fingle
Bridge and WALK 6

WALK 7

1105 ft.
Cranbrook
Castle

Cranbrook

Willingstone

Butterdon

• Monolith

Hill
Farm

Coombe

To Okehampton
← A382

MORETONHAMPSTEAD

† Church

To
Exeter

B3212 to Tavistock
←

N
↑

Not to scale

START — Car Parks
(Both have
Public Lavatories)

banks and ditches on its summit. A quite stupendous view opens out from here, from Exmoor in the north to Hay Tor in the south.

Return 300yd to the track and turn left to the top of the woods where a signposted short cut path right leads back to Cranbrook farm. From this point an extension of one mile downhill to Fingle Bridge, plus of course one mile uphill back, can be made, and this links up with Walk 6. The way down and back is straightforward. There is a restaurant at Fingle Bridge.

Enter the short cut path by a good wood-and-stone stile, reflecting that none of the stone parts of these stiles are likely to be less than 200 years old, and follow the hedge left through two fields to the lane at Cranbrook farm.

Turn left here, walk along the road past the farm, right at the fork and past a large rock bearing a weather vane. 200yd past this rock, turn in right at a signposted stile, and take the lower track of two through a plantation, coming out by a gateless gap into a narrow lane. Walk down here to a minor road, carry straight on, and where the road turns sharp right keep going straight on along a rubble track. When the track bears right towards Hill farm, the path is now steep and rough and green and goes on down towards Coombe, and stays on the track until the penultimate field before Coombe farm, where a 90-degree path sign directs walkers behind the farm to the right. Waymarks here help to identify the actual route which follows the up-slope side of a hedge, and four final stiles in quick succession bring the walker down to a small valley on the outskirts of Moretonhampstead below a council estate.

A brief climb and a left turn and one is back in the town with the feeling that you have taken part in a pedestrian steeplechase!

Walk 8   Steps Bridge to Hel Tor

3½ miles (5.5km)

OS sheet 191

Starting and finishing in valley woodland, this walk climbs to Hel
Tor, a prominent border height on north-east Dartmoor.
  Park your car in the public car park beside the B3212 on the
higher side of Steps Bridge cafe. A Dartmoor National Park
information centre is open from Easter to October.

Cross the road and walk up the long narrow valley-bottom field with
woods on either side. Steps Bridge Youth Hostel is the wooden
building up the hill to your right as you cross the stream near the
road.
  Carry on up the valley crossing the stream once more after ¼ mile.
In another ¼ mile enter a field by a signposted gate and head for an
oak tree by the stream which marks the crossing place of the stream
yet again. Now look out for a waymarked post and path sign and
beyond a waymarked gate. Pass through this gate and follow a
muddy lane through Burnicombe farm. Beyond the farm the route
becomes the main farm approach and is well surfaced.
  Turn right 500yd beyond the farm and 250yd further on look out
for a stile to the right, and a permitted path to Hel Tor. Hel Tor is
one of those uncommon features on Dartmoor, a tor surrounded by
fields, so the National Park Authority has negotiated a fieldside path
to the rock with an explanatory map and details of the access
agreement on display by the stile. If walkers keep to the permitted
path and tor everyone is happy, especially the farmers, who were
tormented by trespassers crossing their fields until this equitable
solution was found.
  From the top there is a fine view of the Dartmoor border country.
The view to the west is interrupted by the foreground, but the two
highest points of the moor, High Willhays and Yes Tor, can just be
seen across the intervening slopes of Mardon.
  Now return to the road, turn right and walk straight for about ¾
mile. This involves turning neither left or right at the crossroads
(Plaston Green) by a large beech tree. But at the first sharp left bend
enter a field to the right by a couple of stiles, follow the hedge/wall
(waymarked) down to a stile at the bottom, and this allows you to
enter a lane leading to the twin farms of Middle and Lower Heltor.
At the foot of the lane and slightly right is a lovely old well, well
worth diverting a few yards to see.
  However, the route from the foot of the lane is straight on through

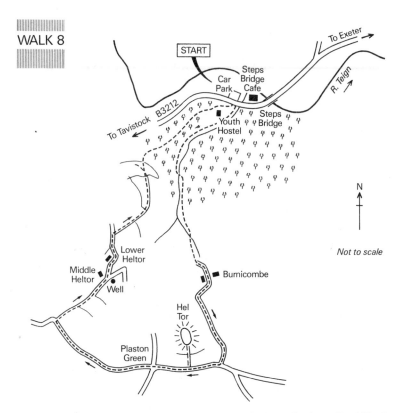

the yard of the second of the two farms and along the lane for 150yd beyond. Turn into a field here through a waymarked gate and follow the right hedge round to the gate at the end of the second field.

From here aim slightly right across a scrubby field for a tree bearing an orange waymark standing beside a gate leading into the wood. Enter the woods, turn right and follow the clear path downwards and back to the B3212–½ mile. The middle section down here is particularly attractive as it follows the spine of a spur, with views on either side through the thin tree cover, and rock showing through the path floor here and there.

Walk 9   Christow and the Three Reservoirs

6 miles (9.5km)

OS sheet 191

This walk is all on tracks and minor roads, and is suitable as a bad weather walk. There are two steep climbs.

Christow is a large village in the Teign valley which, like its neighbours to north and south, Bridford and Hennock, faces east and turns its back on Dartmoor, so to speak. To reach Christow, turn west off the B3193 Teign valley road and park near the church.

From the church, walk uphill for a few yards, then left up Church Lane. Keep straight on when Butts Lane (a reminder of the time when every man had to take part in compulsory archery practice) comes in from the right, then right at Pound where there is a letterbox in the wall. Pass Bennah farm and climb steeply, and take a right fork signposted 'No Through Road' which levels out then climbs again towards Cleave House.

The tarmac road ends at the house, and the right of way enters a wood and bears right (ignore another track left). Then begins a very pleasant section, particularly in early summer when the bluebells are in bloom and the trees are alive with birdsong.

The track now enters Bowden farmyard through a gate, carries on round the outside of the buildings and heads towards the road along the main approach to Bowden, which kinks through 90 degrees a couple of times. On reaching the road, turn left and at the road junction after 200yd take the 'No Through Road', otherwise unsignposted.

Now follows an easy quiet section mostly through conifer plantations. The tarmac road ends opposite Clampitt House, then descends slightly to a junction of tracks where, on the right, a plaque reads:

Society of Friends
Quakers
Clampitt Burial Ground
1670 – 1740

No memorial stones mark the graves. In the days of religious intolerance the Quakers had to meet in secluded parts of the country to escape mob violence.

Turn left here, walk straight to the next 90 degree bend and turn

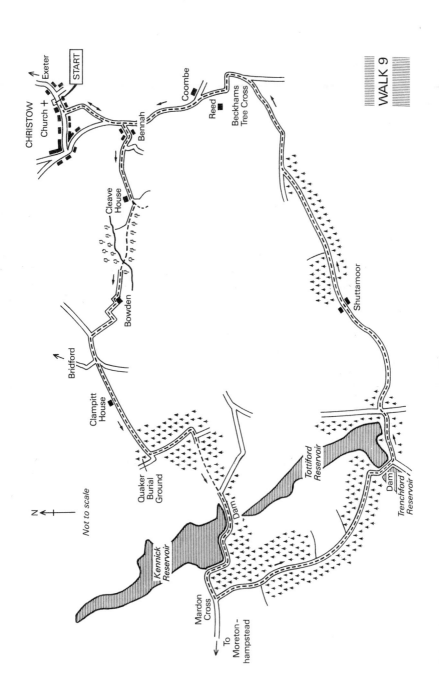

CHRISTOW

Church +
Exeter
START

Bennah
Coombe
Reed
Beckhams
Tree Cross

Cleave
House

Bowden

Bridford

Clampitt
House

Shuttamoor

Quaker Burial
Ground

Kennick
Reservoir

Dam

Tottiford
Reservoir

Dam

Trenchford
Reservoir

Mardon
Cross

To Moreton-
hampstead

N

Not to scale

WALK 9

right here, then leave the rough vehicle track and climb a stile which leads to a path heading gently downhill. The woods are left behind at another stile and the road joined just east of the dam separating Kennick reservoir, 1860 (right) from Tottiford reservoir, 1884, (left). These reservoirs are much used by trout fishermen and make an attractive scene. They were originally built to supply the then fast-growing resort of Torquay.

Keep on the road now as far as Mardon Cross; turn left (signposted 'Bovey') and follow a mostly level road for just over one mile through conifer plantations to the dam between Tottiford reservoir (left) and Trenchford reservoir, 1907 (right). Cross the dam and turn left along a road past a gate which may be marked 'private', but which can be ignored. This road has been opened to the public to improve access round the reservoirs.

At the T-junction at the far end of this link road turn left, then almost immediately right up an unsignposted road which soon levels out and becomes unfenced in places. Unfortunately the level road doesn't last! It plunges steeply down to Shuttamoor farm, then as violently ascends on the other side to a delightful wooded stretch and a general downhill section.

A road joins from the left, but keep straight on, and turn left at the foot of the hill at Beckhams Tree Cross. Look out just round a big bend for the spoil tips on your left of a nineteenth-century lead mine at Reed farm. During much of last century many mines were worked in this valley and some continued until recent years. The barytes mine at Bridford closed in 1958 and the Great Rock micaceous haematite mine at Hennock closed in 1969.

Keep left at Combe and the way back to Christow is now clear and signposted, a walk of about ¾ mile.

Walk 10   Lustleigh Cleave

3 miles (4.8km)

OS sheet 191

This is a footpath walk through tumbled border country, with a steep climb early on.

Park your car near Lustleigh church, which is ¾ mile off the A382, three miles north of Bovey Tracey.

Lustleigh is an attractive village with old houses mixed up with some modern bungalows. A feature of the locality are the large pudding-shaped rocks which seem to have burst out of the ground. The church is a typical moorland sanctuary with a good sixteenth-century screen and an early Christian memorial stone which for hundreds of years was used as the threshold to the church. It was moved in 1979 to prevent further wear.

Leave the village centre by walking up past the Cleave Hotel to the parish war memorial. Turn left here, still uphill, and almost immediately left along a private unmade road (signposted). At the end of the road, beside a large house, pass through a kissing gate into a sloping field. This is the Lustleigh church path, the regular way for parishioners up the valley to reach the village centre hundreds of years ago.

Follow the upper path which contours the slope below a large rock, and at the end of the field at another kissing gate and signpost take the middle path of three choices and head for the bottom of the woods ahead. The course is now clear and uncomplicated until Lower Combe is reached. Turn left beside the house, taking the left track heading for the stream which is crossed by a small clapper bridge. Now turn left over a stile, then right and climb progressively steeper up a well waymarked path through a woodland jungle.

A stile brings one out into the road where you turn left for 25yd, then right up a narrow lane between properties called Grove and North Park. This brings one to a gate, path junction and signpost where a left fork is taken, keeping to the wall more or less closely through attractive open woodland with many scattered rocks. About 10yd before the highest point turn right and climb up a less well worn path through trees to the summit of Sharpitor, one of Dartmoor's ten Sharp Tors. (This section can be hard to follow when the bracken is high.)

It is an idiosyncrasy of Dartmoor speech that a vowel is often inserted between consonants. Thus, Sharp Tor becomes Sharpitor;

37

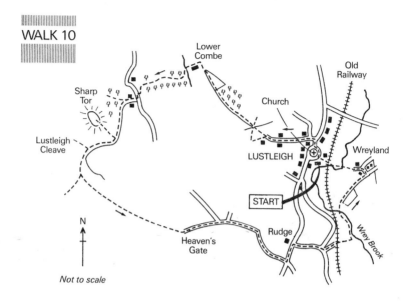

WALK 10

Lower Combe

Old Railway

Sharp Tor

Church

Lustleigh Cleave

Wreyland

LUSTLEIGH

START

N

Rudge

Wrey Brook

Heaven's Gate

Not to scale

Broad Marsh and Broad Falls become Broadamarsh or Broadymarsh and Broadafalls.

A fine view opens out from here across Lustleigh Cleave extending to left and right in the foreground, with the river Bovey at the bottom. Manaton church tower may be picked out due west, with the great rounded hill of Hameldon beyond. Hound Tor is the prominent tor a little to the south.

The rocky eminence on which you are standing once bore a naturally-balanced stone famed for its ability to crack nuts, and called the Nutcracker. Unfortunately it was yanked 60ft over the edge with a crow-bar by two inebriated vandals about 30 years ago and was damaged in the fall so that the efforts of the Royal Engineers to replace it came to naught. The name Nutcracker persists on most modern maps.

Because it is no longer regularly grazed the character of the Cleave has changed, even in my lifetime. It used to be much more open in character, but before long it will be woodland, at least on the lower slopes.

Now return to the main path and continue on and down taking Heaven's Gate as the next objective at signposts, which means bearing left at path junctions. You should keep left, south, and after nearly one mile you reach a gate. This was christened Heaven's Gate as the view across the Cleave for anyone coming out of the gate evoked feelings of paradise. But as indicated earlier, the nature of the Cleave has changed, and trees now screen the sweep of landscape. Enter the gate, follow the lane to the road, turn right and walk down to Rudge Cross. Turn left here, and right opposite Rudge farm after 50yd. At the foot of this short lane turn left and after 30yd right down a track through the demolished arch of the Moretonhampstead railway branch line (opened 1866, closed 1959).

The path now skirts two sides of the village sewage works, crosses the Wrey (or Wray) Brook by a footbridge, then bears left for 100yd before passing in front of a large boulder and climbing behind it to a gate. Follow the right field edge to another gate and into a lane leading to the beautiful hamlet of Wreyland (or Wrayland). Turn left, and the road, which degenerates into a track, leads back to Lustleigh past the cricket pitch and a brick chapel.

Anyone wanting to learn more about Wreyland and Lustleigh should read the three volumes of *Small Talk at Wreyland* by Cecil Torr, which he published between 1918 and 1923 and which were reprinted in one volume in 1970. It is a delightful journey into the past; a truly relaxing bedside book.

Walk 11   The Lower Bovey Valley and Shap Tor

5½ miles (9km)

OS sheet 191

This is a mixed walk of woods and field paths, with a few minor roads. There are two steep climbs.

Park your car in either of the two public car parks in Bovey Tracey which stands at the crossing of the A382 and B3344.

Bovey Tracey is a lively little town, with an economy now mostly dependent on commuters, retired people and holidaymakers, although the handsome converted riverside mill is now occupied by an industrial enterprise. The church is one of the finest in the Dartmoor area with a glorious screen and pulpit, and various other interesting fittings,. The Dartmoor National Park headquarters, standing in beautiful grounds on the Hay Tor road at Parke, was opened in the summer of 1979. The house was built in 1828 by the Hole family, and lived in by them until Major Hole died in 1974 aged 93.

From the centre of Bovey Tracey, by the horse trough, walk behind the Cromwell Arms and through the Cromwell Arch (a ruin of uncertain antecedents, but older than Cromwell's day) and along a road of Cornish Unit houses to the far end.

This is a walk with an inauspicious beginning, and it is hard to imagine as one approaches the turning circle at the end that a narrow footway here will take you behind and beyond the estate to a pleasant path on the fringe of the town.

Take the cut, and turn right along a footpath looking out for Parke, the Dartmoor National Park headquarters, through the trees to your left. On reaching a lane, turn left and pass through the yard of Southbrook farm aiming for the left side of the hedge facing you where there is a stile.

Follow the hedge to tne woods, and enter them by a stile. These are glorious beech woods, best seen in spring or autumn. The path is clear and direct. Another stile is reached, giving access to a field across which the path runs to the far end where there is another stile. The path now runs along the side of a steep slope above the track of the disused Moretonhampstead branch line (opened 1866, closed 1959) before briefly entering the field above, which it leaves at the bottom corner for a steep drop down to the road near Wilford Bridge.

Now pass through the arch of the disused railway, and turn right

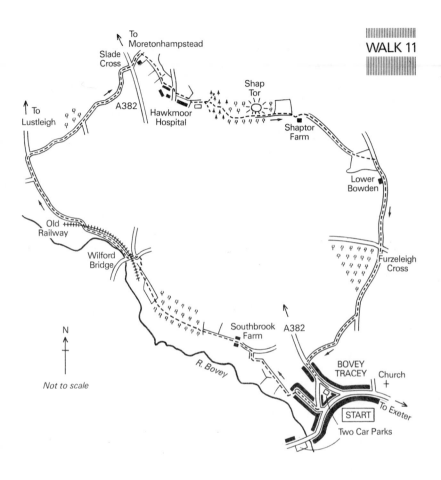

To Moretonhampstead

Slade Cross

To Lustleigh

A382

Hawkmoor Hospital

Shap Tor

Shaptor Farm

Lower Bowden

Old Railway

Wilford Bridge

Furzeleigh Cross

Southbrook Farm

A382

R. Bovey

N

Not to scale

BOVEY TRACEY

Church

To Exeter

START

Two Car Parks

along the Lustleigh road for ⅔ mile. Along here on the left there was for a time in the 1920s and 1930s a stopping place on the railway called Hawkmoor Halt, and the gate leading to it is still visible, though overgrown. This was a response to the presence of the sanatorium over the hill to the east which you will soon see, but was some distance from it.

About 200yd past a turning signposted 'Manaton' turn up right, and after 10yd take the rough track climbing left. This meets Hatherleigh Lane at the entrance to Higher Knowle nature reserve. From here follow the undulating road straight on to Slade Cross on the A382. Along here the straggling buildings of Hawkmoor Hospital can be seen on the west-facing hillside. This grew up as Devon's tuberculosis hospital earlier this century.

At Slade Cross take the Hennock road, noting the old stone direction post by the letterbox, and 80yd up turn in right at a footpath signpost. The path is waymarked. Pass through the gate into rough land and along the top edge of two fields but outside them at the foot of a bramble slope. Enter a small gate, cross to a larger gate and walk along a cinder track beside a hospital block. Cross a lane, walk down slightly and go into a field, following the bottom hedge. Pass through the gate at the end, go down a few yards and over a stile into a narrow field above a tennis court. Turn left here (signposted) then pick up a track leading into the woods.

At a fork of grassy tracks turn left, then right after five yards up through conifers. Cross a bulldozed track, past a Hawkmoor Water Supply notice bearing a waymark and climb steeply. The path is narrow and enters Woodland Trust land.

Buzzards may be heard overhead, and around one in the woods are fenced-off shaft openings, so keep to the path. It is well marked and continues to climb. Opposite the highest point of the path left is a large slab of rock, Shap Tor. Make your own way to the summit. The view westwards is quite magnificent and encompasses the highest points of Dartmoor. The skirts of the tor are bedecked with bluebells in May.

Return to the path and follow it along a green track and over stiles past Shap Tor farm. Now follow a grassy lane which becomes an avenue and leads into a field. From the gate make for the highest part of the field where a wood and stone stile leads into the road. Turn right and follow the road back to Bovey Tracey, one mile away.

Walk 12

3 miles (4.8km)

Grimspound (from the east) and Hameldon

OS sheet 191

This is an open moor walk to a Bronze Age village, also visiting a Bronze Age cairn. This walk should not be attempted in mist unless you are accomplished in map and compass work.

Park your car by the roadside at Natsworthy Gate (grid ref. 721802). This is on a little-used minor road, and it may be reached by driving either 2½ miles up the valley road from Widecombe, or taking the uphill road for one mile from Heatree Cross on the B3344. Natsworthy Gate is at the top end of a fine beech avenue. A signpost gives footpath and bridleway directions.

From the gate giving access to the open moor on the west of the road follow the broad path up the hillside towards the top corner of the wall on your right. From here a prominent pointed stone becomes visible on the skyline. Make for it. You will find it bears the following inscription:

†
R A F
S49
R D W
C J L
R B
R L A E
21. 3. 41

The stone is a memorial to the crew of a Handley Page Hampden bomber, 'S' of 49 Squadron, which crashed here on its way back from operations. The names of the dead crew were Wilson, Lyon, Branes and Ellis, and the stone was erected at the request of the mother of Pilot Officer the Hon R.D.Wilson.

Before leaving the stone glance south to the small but steep valley of the East Webburn. This will be the route back to the gate at the end of the walk.

Now return to the main path, slightly north of where you are now, and follow it westwards. The scattered poles are another reminder of the war. They were stuck up to deter enemy gliders from landing, and those that remain have defied forty years of Dartmoor weather and use by animals as rubbing posts.

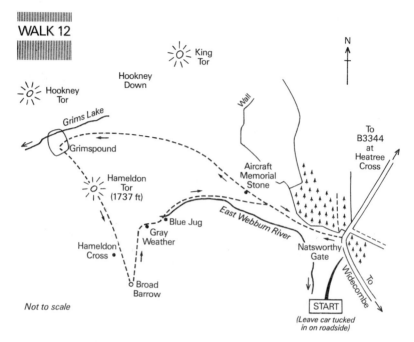

WALK 12

King Tor

Hookney Down

Hookney Tor

Grims Lake

Grimspound

Hameldon Tor (1737 ft)

Wall

To B3344 at Heatree Cross

Aircraft Memorial Stone

Blue Jug

Gray Weather

Hameldon Cross •

East Webburn River

Natsworthy Gate

To Widecombe

Broad Barrow

Not to scale

N

START

(Leave car tucked in on roadside)

As the path begins to descend, the scars of mine workings become visible ahead. This track was the mine workers' route to Manaton at weekends. During the week they lived at the mine.

About 1½ miles from Natsworthy Gate the ruined wall of Grimspound is reached. It is a west-facing village site of about four acres with many ruined stone huts, some of which were probably stores or animal pens. The entrance to the enclosure was on the higher side, giving access to the high pastures of Hameldon, surely a clue to the economy of the inhabitants, and the indefensible site of Grimspound at a time of slings, arrows and spears, overlooked as it is on two sides, must mean that the people who lived there were peaceful folk. The wall was built to keep wild animals out and domestic animals in. The walls of two huts have been conjecturally restored. See how the stream, the Grims Lake, ran through the enclosure. However, it was not a reliable water source as it dries up in drought conditions. The site could have been occupied any time between 2000 BC and 700 BC.

From here climb the steep hill to the south to Hameldon Tor (1737ft), which is disappointing as a tor but splendid as a viewpoint, particularly to the west and north. The whole of this great hill which extends southwards for a couple of miles is referred to as Hameldon.

Continue south along a slight dip, and the remains of Hameldon Cross become visible a few yards from the path right. It bears an inscription 'HC DS 1854'. The DS stands for the Duke of Somerset who owned the land in 1854 and who marked his boundary with a series of stones bearing his initials, and the names of the stones. Now head for Broad Barrow, a Bronze Age burial cairn to the south-east. This bears another 'DS' stone inscribed 'Broad Burrow' on its top. From here follow a galloping track north for 400yd to a dip in the land, and turn north-east here into a shallow depression which is the head of the East Webburn. A boundary stone, inscribed 'Gray Weather' with a stone beside it, is to be found at the north-west limit of rushes, and another, the 'Blue Jug' is further down the slope in the middle of rushes, and about 200yd east-north-east. This is a delightful upland side-valley, and a good place to come to find peace. The only man-made noises are likely to be high-flying aircraft. Look out for red grouse around here as this is good heather country, and they feed on heather shoots.

Trace the tiny stream down, keeping about halfway up the slope. When the first trees are reached in the valley the start of the walk at Natsworthy Gate becomes visible ahead. Head for it downhill.

Walk 13   Hay Tor and the Granite Tramway

3 miles (4.8km)

OS sheet 191

An easy open-country walk across border moorland provided the weather is clear, this provides a suitable introduction to Dartmoor for newcomers.

Leave your car in the car park on the highest part of the road four miles west of Bovey Tracey in the south-east corner of Dartmoor. Hay Tor is signposted from Bovey Tracey. There are public lavatories at the foot of the hill.

From the car park walk up the gentle grassy slope towards the right hand rock of Hay Tor. You will see that from this side the lump you are aiming for is the dominant feature. From the north this influence is reversed.

Halfway to the rock from the road look out for a rock perched on a couple of small stones standing on the edge of the bracken area. Peer underneath and you will see it has been worked to a smooth surface, but presumably a fault developed and after being half completed as an edge runner for some sort of crusher it was rejected. I wonder how many of the people who pass it realise what it is?

The tor can be climbed, but anyone with slippery footwear or lacking a head for heights is advised not to make the ascent. There is a wide gap to cross near the top and the rudimentary steps cut in the rock can be treacherous. From the summit, 1490ft, a fine view can be obtained. On a clear day you can see across to Princetown on western Dartmoor which is backed by North Hessary Tor and its BBC television mast. Exmoor may be seen as a blue blur to the north, and the Teign estuary is conspicuous in the other direction. The white scars in the valley to the east are ball clay workings. At your feet notice the large white felspar crystals which are one of the three constituents of granite, the others being mica and quartz.

Now carefully descend and go down the path towards the quarry spoil tips visible to the north-east. When you reach the edge of the inner quarry you will see it contains two deep pools, and the scene is one of beauty and tranquillity. Scramble down into the quarry by one of several paths or come into it through the entrance. A fallen derrick lies half in the water and if you are lucky you may spot goldfish in the deeper of the two ponds. They manage to escape the depredations of visiting herons, presumably because of the depth of the water. Dragonflies skim the surface. The quarry was worked

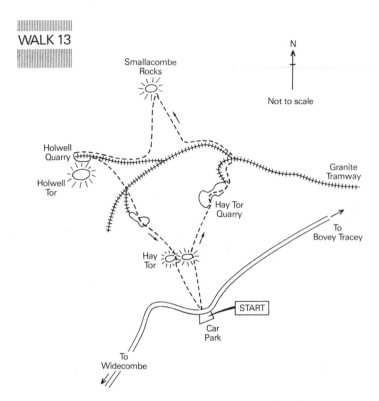

Smallacombe
Rocks

N

Not to scale

Holwell
Quarry

Granite
Tramway

Holwell
Tor

Hay Tor
Quarry

To
Bovey Tracey

Hay
Tor

START

Car
Park

To
Widecombe

from about 1820 to 1860 and stone was sent to London for many public buildings.

Move out of the inner quarry. The outer, lower level quarry is passed and a cutting giving acess to this one should be followed, and its track traced round to the left beneath tips of waste rock. At this point you will notice two parallel lines of grooved stone blocks like railway lines, which is what in fact they were. Keep following them away from the quarry where they bear round to the right across a broken embankment, and the quarry branch line soon meets the 'main' line at a spot where the stone blocks form a set of junction points.

This is the famous granite tramway which was used from about 1825 to 1858. Stone was loaded onto flat-top, wooden-wheeled trucks pulled by horses which took the stone eight miles down into the valley where it was transferred to barges for conveyance to Teignmouth and loading into sea-going vessels. This double transhipment made the quarry uneconomical to work. The system reverses the normal railway technique which has the flange on the wheels and employs simple rails. Here the retaining flange was on

47

the rails, or sets, and the material was available for the cost of extraction.

Follow the tramway up a slight gradient, round a gulley and into a cutting. When it comes out of the cutting and heads straight for Holwell Tor leave the tramway and head north-west across level ground for Smallacombe Rocks, a tor in all but name. It is incorrectly called Grea Tor on maps, but Grea Tor is the much larger feature halfway up the other side of the valley. Beside Smallacombe Rocks on the east side are the ruins of several prehistoric huts.

Soak in the view from here. Hound Tor is the huge tor to the west and the Becky (Becka) Brook flows down the valley. Listen, and you may hear the 'cronk cronk' of a raven, and maybe the sound of wing beats will first alert you to the presence overhead of these large black birds.

The next place to visit is Holwell quarry whose rock face is visible across the small combe (hence the name of these rocks) to the south-west. Don't take a direct course as marshy ground intervenes; instead follow a path in line with Hay Tor, and after 300yd veer off right towards the granite tramway where it ran down to Holwell quarry. This is the haunt of the stonechat; listen for its metallic call.

As you approach the quarries a ruined blacksmith's shop is seen left, and soon the sheer vertical face of the main quarry. Past this and on the lower side of the tramway is a well-preserved workmen's shelter with its roof still intact.

Retrace your steps along the granite tramway for 150yd and mount the path to the right just before a wet section by a few rowan trees. Where this path levels out make for yet another quarry straight ahead in line with Hay Tor. This one rejoices in the name of Rubble Heap. Note how the westerly lump of Hay Tor has now achieved supremacy. Walk into the quarry, scramble up the easy path at the back and head for the larger block of Hay Tor. This part of the moor produces masses of succulent whortleberries in August. The tor can be climbed with the aid of iron hand-holds, and is in fact higher than its more frequently climbed sibling, Now head downhill back to the car.

Stone stile at
beginning of
Butterdon path
(Walk 7)

The Hall House, Wreyland, Lustleigh (Walk 10)

Postbridge, the clapper bridge, with the road bridge behind
(Walk 16)

Vixen Tor
(Walk 25)

Walk 14

3½ miles (5.5km)

OS sheet 191

Widecombe-in-the-Moor to Thorneyhill Lane and Bonehill

This walk is mostly on quiet country roads, but with one steep rough section. It could be followed by parents with a push chair.

Widecombe-in-the-Moor is reached by following the signs from the B3344 at Bovey Tracey or by turning off the B3357 at Poundsgate. Park in the village car park.

Widecombe has achieved through its fair and song the sort of fame (some might say notoriety) which few small country villages possess. Grasmere (Wordsworth), Oare (the Doones), Polperro and Castle Combe (quaintness), Stoke Poges (Gray's *Elegy*) and Selborne (Gilbert White) are other places which for literary and landscape reasons have this power to attract.

Certainly the village has a superb valley site, and the church tower is the finest on Dartmoor, drawing the eye from all points of the compass. The far-flung parish too has many features of interest for the discerning visitor; numerous old stone farms, isolated patches of moorland, valley woods, prehistoric remains, tors and rocks.

In the large church look out for the fragments of the medieval rood screen, and in the base of the tower the rustic verses describing the great storm of 1638 when lightning struck the tower, causing some of the masonry to fall into the church and killing several worshippers.

The church house is the nearest building to the tower, and is now the parish hall. In its time – and it was built about 1550, if not before – it has been brewhouse, almshouse, poorhouse and school. The village green was once the local archery training ground. Just below the post office is the village well. It's not advisable to use it as drinking water.

Widecombe Fair is held annually on the second Tuesday in September. A one-way traffic system operates as so many people want to come, and it really is a worthwhile experience. There are animal classes, show jumping, sideshows, stalls, a small funfair and someone dressed up as Uncle Tom Cobleigh. The young men have a race to the top of Widecombe Hill and back.

The village sign was designed by Lady Sayer, a local resident, to replace an earlier one destroyed when signs were suppressed during the war.

From the green, leave the village by the thatched tea hut and follow the unsignposted road up the valley heading towards Natsworthy.

49

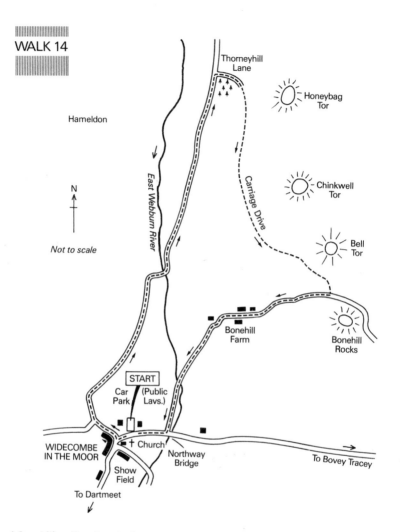

WALK 14

Thorneyhill Lane

Honeybag Tor

Hameldon

East Webburn River

N

Not to scale

Carriage Drive

Chinkwell Tor

Bell Tor

Bonehill Farm

Bonehill Rocks

START

Car Park

(Public Lavs.)

WIDECOMBE IN THE MOOR

† Church

Northway Bridge

To Bovey Tracey

Show Field

To Dartmeet

After 1½ miles, just before a cattle grid, turn steeply up right. This is Thorneyhill Lane, and it leads to a pleasant open level carriage drive which contours south below Honeybag Tor and Chinkwell Tor with glorious views across and down the valley.

At the next road, turn right down Bonehill, passing the fine group of Bonehill farms. At the T-junction turn right, and the village is reached in 200yd.

Walk 15

6½ miles (10.5km)

Leusdon, Dr Blackall's Drive and Spitchwick

OS sheets 191 and 202

This is a varied walk with open moor, field paths and riverside walk. It has a not very severe climb at the end.

Leave your car on the grassy triangle near Leusdon church, Leusdon Common. To find Leusdon, turn off the B3357 at Poundsgate along the Widecombe road, then right by a large monolith erected to mark the 1977 Silver Jubilee.

Walk west along the wide level road with the West Webburn in the valley to your right. After 900yd, turn up left through Sweaton farm (signposted), and follow the muddy lane uphill. At the top of the lane, follow the signposted instruction to walk on the right of the hedge. At the top of this field pass through the gate to the other side, continue upwards and exit to the lane by a stile.

Turn right along this minor road, then up left when the open moor is reached, keeping outside the enclosures. Make initially for a wall corner marked by a prominent thorn tree just beyond a domestic water supply (leat) running north–south. Now bear slightly left and head for the next wall corner. Leave the wall at 45 degrees and you should reach the B3357 at Bel Tor Corner where there is a parking space opposite, and where the road ceases to be enclosed.

There is a fine view from here taking in North Hessary Tor in the west (with its BBC television mast) to Hay Tor in the east, and even Fernworthy Forest can be seen peeping over a ridge away to the north.

Now follow the wall heading south towards Mel Tor. Bel Tor, left, is imprisoned among enclosures, and Venford reservoir twinkles (if the sun is shining!) 1½ miles away across the Dart valley. Jink with the track between the walls. This is the beginning of Dr Blackall's Drive, which that gentleman laid out about a hundred years ago so that he could view the scenery from the comfort of his carriage.

When the track debouches on to the open moor, bear slightly right and climb to Mel Tor to get a better appreciation of the view. Across the valley is the long rib of Bench Tor, and beneath your feet on the summit are some well shaped rock basins (natural).

Now return to the drive, and follow it along. At Brake Corner the underlying granite is left behind and the blue elvan comes to the surface. The hill farmer has cause to be grateful for the presence of

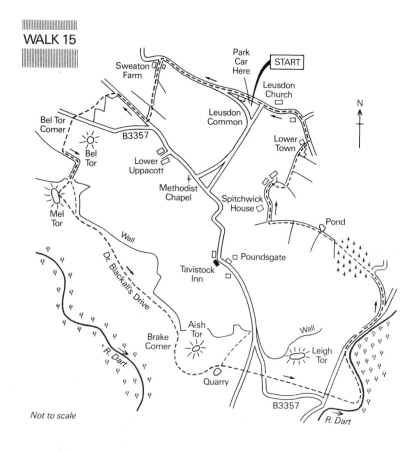

START

Park
Car
Here

Sweaton
Farm

Leusdon
Church

Leusdon
Common

Bel Tor
Corner

Lower
Town

B3357

Bel
Tor

Lower
Uppacott

Methodist
Chapel

Spitchwick
House

Mel
Tor

Pond

Wall

Dr. Blackall's Drive

Poundsgate

Tavistock
Inn

Aish
Tor

Wall

Brake
Corner

Leigh
Tor

R. Dart

Quarry

B3357

N

R. Dart

Not to scale

the elvan as ruminant animals grazing upon its slopes don't suffer
from 'moorsick' as animals do in granite country. This illness is
caused by a cobalt deficiency.

As the drive bears round left below Aish Tor a spiky tor comes
into view ahead – Leigh Tor. Then a quarry with tatty posts and
wire is passed below the drive to the right. From here make directly
for the river which is visible looping round a grassy strath ½ mile
away. You will cross three roads before you reach the river.

When you reach the Dart follow it downstream. Note how in
places the Dartmoor National Park Authority has restored the left
bank where it was suffering from human erosion. This was a pioneer
effort, with the gang experimenting as they proceeded, but the work
seems to be holding up. Where the river meets the road, get on the
road and follow it for 350yd to a fork where you should turn up left
(signposted 'Lower Town').

At a sharp bend to the right and beside some cottages, continue straight up a track between conifer plantations. The path is waymarked and clear. It leaves the wood, follows the bottom of three fields and meets a private road near Spitchwick House. Turn right here and follow the road (it is a public right of way) to a signposted gate (right) into a field. Now head for the second gate on the left and follow the hedge to Lower Town. At Lower Town, turn left and follow the minor road back to Leusdon Common up a fairly steep hill.

Walk 16   Up the East Dart River from Postbridge
6 or 7 miles (9.5 or 11km)

OS sheet 191

This route is over open moor; it should not be attempted in bad weather unless you are accomplished in map and compass work.

Postbridge is on the B3212, and just about in the middle of the Dartmoor National Park. There is a large car park, public lavatories, a petrol station, a shop and post office, and a pub. A Dartmoor National Park information centre is open between Easter and October.

Whether you approach Postbridge from the east or west, but especially from the east, it has the appearance of an oasis in the desert. There are plenty of walk possibilities from here, and that given below is one of many. Postbridge developed in the late eighteenth and early nineteenth centuries, but never came to much. The road south to Bellever was only opened in the 1930s when the Forestry Commission started to plant the slopes of Lakehead Hill and Bellever Tor. The clapper bridge will be noticed towards the end of the walk.

Leave the car park by the stiles in the top corner, and turn right along Drift Lane. This is the broad path between the Archerton enclosures (left) and the East Dart river, and was the route by which cattle were driven to and from the open moor. A drift on Dartmoor means a round-up of animals.

Follow Drift Lane to its northern end where a gate (see cover photograph) gives access to a newtake, an area of enclosed moor. Keep on the gently rising track keeping the wall on your right, but after 100yd leave the track and stick with the wall as the track deviates left. Trace the wall to the Broad Down Brook and cross it where two branches of this stream come together at a spot where there is a broken wall. Now climb steeply to a stile up and to your right.

Having crossed the stile you will find you are on a bank with what appears to be a ditch to your left. The ditch is the dried-up course of the Powder Mills leat which drew water from the East Dart and ran it along the contours on a steadily falling course to the place between Postbridge and Two Bridges where gunpowder was made in the last century. The water operated waterwheels for the various manufacturing processes.

If it seems strange to have had such an industry on the moor, it

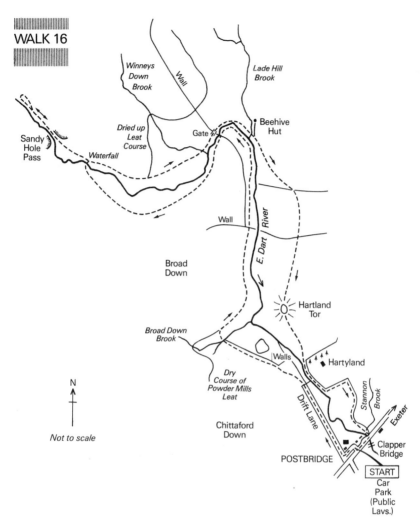

Winneys
Down
Brook

Wall

Lade Hill
Brook

Beehive
Hut

Dried up
Leat
Course

Gate

Sandy
Hole
Pass

Waterfall

Wall

E. Dart River

Broad
Down

Hartland
Tor

Broad Down
Brook

Walls

Hartyland

Dry
Course of
Powder Mills
Leat

N

Stannon Brook

Exeter

Drift Lane

Not to scale

Chittaford
Down

Clapper
Bridge

POSTBRIDGE

START
Car
Park
(Public
Lavs.)

must be pointed out that water power was cheap, stone for building was ready to hand, space for safety was plentiful and even labour was easy to come by at that time. Like so many Dartmoor projects it had a short life. The ruins of the mills and chimneys can be seen north of the B3212, but are invisible from here as Chittaford Down intervenes. The cottages are still occupied.

Follow the leat bank for nearly a mile to where the leat was taken off the East Dart, and continue up the right bank, crossing a stile, picking your way along sheep tracks and making the best route across what becomes a steep slope, where the river runs rapidly down a gorge-like valley. Here it is sensible to stay up fairly high.

At the top of the gorge, the river changes direction, so we follow it round, and 200yd from the bend reach a waterfall. The river can be crossed here, except after heavy rain when it must not be attempted. In this case the outward route back should be used.

From here it is possible to extend the walk for one mile by following up the left bank for ½ mile to the top end of Sandy Hole Pass. This feature is a narrow defile through which the river runs after leaving Broada Marsh which is the flat area upstream from the Pass. Sandy Hole Pass can be seen as the narrow valley ¼ mile up-river from the waterfall.

The suggestion is that the walker goes as far as the upstream end to view the wilderness scene from that point. There is no problem in route-finding so long as the river is not lost sight of. Between the waterfall and Sandy Hole Pass you will pass a ruined tinners' hut standing among the debris of tin workings. Where the river runs through Sandy Hole Pass notice how its channel has been deepened and the sides built up. This was to quicken the flow and lower the watertable in the marshy area upstream, the better to work the tin-bearing gravels there.

The return walk from the waterfall starts by following the bank of another leat on the left bank. This one was about seven or eight miles long and took water to the mines near the Warren House Inn to work the waterwheels. After 250yd look below right for a tree 15yd below the bank where the leat bends round to the left. At this point leave the bank and head down the hillside on a line with the forest corner in the distance, then aim for a crossing point on the small side-stream ahead, the Winney's Down Brook, 50yd up from its confluence with the East Dart. There is a small ford here.

Now follow a track to the hunting gate in the newtake wall ahead, staying on the path and passing an occupied rabbit warren. Bear right above the right angle bend of the river and cross the next stream, the Lade Hill Brook, where convenient. A curious structure, the well-known beehive hut of unknown date, may be found in a gulley on the east side of this stream 80yd up from where it falls into the Dart.

Now climb the hill slantwise and follow the ridge parallel to the river and opposite to our outward route. One wall has to be crossed, but there is a convenient gate on the east side of the ridge which should be used.

Head for Hartland Tor ahead, then drop down and aim for the point where the conifer shelter belt belonging to Hartyland meets the river. There is a path here which gets one past the field in front of the house. Upon reaching the rough pasture just north of Post-bridge, turn left along a wall (signposted) then right along the next wall, and the road is reached by the bridge.

Cross the bridge (mind the traffic!) and have a look at the clapper bridge just downstream. These bridges are hard to date, and may not be as old as they look. This one is the best on the moor and was probably built in the thirteenth century. One can only marvel at their ability to withstand flood water. I have seen a photograph showing a torrent lapping the underneath of the horizontal spans!

The car park is now just a stone's throw away.

Walk 17   Bellever and the East Dart River
3 miles (4.8km)

OS sheet 191

This is an easy walk with no steep climbs, but if the river is running fast the stepping stones at the halfway point should not be attempted.

Bellever is a Forestry Commission hamlet with a Youth Hostel, built round an ancient farm. It is reached along a minor road one mile south of the B3212 at Postbridge in the middle of the moor. The tree-screened car park is between the houses and the river. There are public lavatories.

From the car park walk back 200yd to the tarmac road and turn right towards the bridge over the East Dart. From the bridge the earlier clapper bridge can be seen just downstream with an incomplete line of stepping stones beyond.

William Crossing wrote (*Amid Devonia's Alps*, 1888, reprinted 1974) that he knew the man who admitted to having thrown off the missing central stone 'when a boy'. Apart from the feat of strength this would have been for a boy, even allowing for an understanding of rock manipulation we have largely forgotten, there is no trace of the dislodged stone. But there is the existing evidence of six mortises (grooves), three on each pier, which could have provided a secure lodgement for three wooden cross pieces which themselves supported a gangway of wooden slats. This seems a much more likely explanation for the missing span.

Cross the bridge and walk down the east (left) bank. The forest, which stretches away in every direction except over Riddon Ridge to the east, began to be planted in 1931. Most of the trees are different varieties of spruce. In the 1960s the Forestry Commission established the car park and a picnic site on the river bank where the Cranery stream falls into the East Dart. As you walk along you will see that the National Park Authority has had to rebuild the river banks here because of erosion from people pressure.

Stay on the river bank and climb a broken wall into Snaily House plantation. After 100yd a ruin will be seen among the trees to your left. This is Whiteslade, or Snaily House as it has come to be known.

Many years ago in that hazy era known as 'once upon a time' the local people were puzzled as to how the two elderly spinsters who lived here managed to look so well fed while keeping no animals and tending no garden. Perhaps they were stealing others' sheep, it was

58

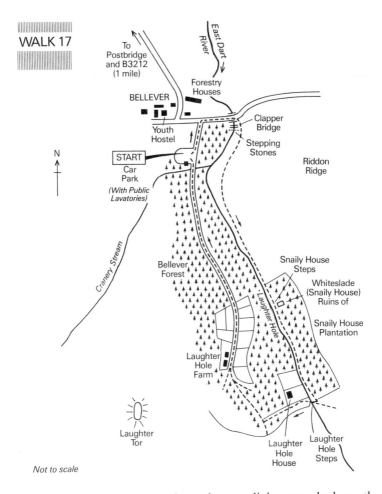

To
Postbridge
and B3212
(1 mile)

East Dart River

Forestry
Houses

BELLEVER

N

Youth
Hostel

Clapper
Bridge

Stepping
Stones

Riddon
Ridge

START
Car
Park
*(With Public
Lavatories)*

Cranery Stream

Bellever
Forest

Snaily House
Steps

Whiteslade
(Snaily House)
Ruins of

Laughter Hole

Snaily House
Plantation

Laughter
Hole
Farm

Laughter
Tor

Laughter
Hole
House

Laughter
Hole
Steps

Not to scale

suggested! So a watch was kept, but no light was shed on the problem. Eventually a deputation marched up to the door, was admitted and got the answer; rows of pans containing slugs pickled in salt. Their secret out, the women pined away and died, and the house sank into ruin. This happened early last century.

When the house was lived in some way of crossing the river was required, and Snaily House stepping stones can be seen in the river opposite the ruin.

Carry on down the left bank and notice the storm-damaged trees along here. The blizzards of 1978 and 1979 wrought great havoc in the Dartmoor forests.

This stretch of the river is called Laughter Hole, from the tor of that name, Laughter Tor, up the hill to the west, and a 'hole' on

Dartmoor is a steep-sided narrow valley. At the foot of the steepest section is Laughter Hole House, built between the wars, and one of the most isolated dwellings on the moor still inhabited, although there is an associated farm not far away which you pass on the way back.

At the southern end of Snaily House plantation cross to the west bank using Laughter Hole stepping stones and follow the way-marked path round the outside of the house garden to a gate leading into the forest. Walk 200yd up this path, turn right at a sign reading 'Bellever' and follow this track for one mile back to the car park. Laughter Hole farm and its fields stands in the middle of the forest and is passed on the way.

Walk 18   Dartmeet to Combestone Tor

3 miles (4.8km)

OS sheets 191 and 202

A long but fairly gentle climb to start, and two lines of slippery stepping stones make this a walk for well-shod, fit people even though it's not long. The stepping stones should not be attempted if the river is running high.

Dartmeet is a popular beauty spot on the Ashburton to Two Bridges road, the B3357. There is a large restaurant.

From the vast car park, walk across the bridge noting the storm-ruined clapper bridge just upstream. The actual meeting point of the two Dart rivers, the East and West, is just downstream from here, and many of the visitors never see it. The united river is sometimes called the Double Dart.

Pass through the forecourt of Dartmeet Service Station and 20yd down a signposted path to a gate. Enter the field, turn left and cross the West Dart by a line of stepping stones. From the south bank follow the path indicated by the signpost up through a pleasant mixture of trees and rocks to a gate leading into a field. Keep beside the left-hand wall making for a gap in the wall ahead, and go through the gap still keeping the wall on your left.

Abreast of Combestone farm a signpost points the way uphill, still beside the wall, to a gate beside a black shed. Go through this gate, now following the farm track to the next gate where the open moor is reached. Mark this spot, as after a visit to Combestone Tor which is visible 400yd ahead we will return here.

Now head for Combestone Tor (pronounced 'Cumston') striding or jumping a leat (artificial watercourse) on the way. A dry leat is just beyond.

At the tor climb to the top of one of the rock piles for a good view. To the south of the tor the high land of southern Dartmoor swells up, broken by the valley of the O Brook, the shortest placename in England. Across the valley to the north, pick out the ruined prehistoric parallel field banks on the facing hillside. At your feet each summit pile has naturally-eroded 'basins' in its surface; a testament to the severity of the weather over millions of years.

Now return to the gate on the farm track, pass through it, and bear left as indicated by the sign reading 'Bridlepath to Week Ford stepping stones'. At the time of writing this next section as far as the river is not well defined.

WALK 18

START

Car Park

R. Dart E.

B3357
Ashburton

DARTMEET

Dartmeet
Stepping Stones

R. Dart

Two Bridges

Combestone
Farm

Combestone
Tor

W. Dart River

To Holne

Week Ford
Stepping Stones

Saddle
Bridge

O Brook

Blowing
Houses

Huccaby or
Hexworthy Bridge

N

Not to scale

First, follow a narrow gulley down the hillside within the wall. This leads to a waymarked gate at the bottom of the field. Pass through here, carry on across a wide culvert and bear slightly right beside a low wall. Now, in the absence of indicators near at hand, head to the right of Huccaby Meadows in the valley beyond, or towards a prominent asbestos-roofed barn at Hexworthy. Either course will get you down to the West Dart.

Now follow the river up, pass through a hunting gate, cross the O Brook at its confluence with the West Dart, and Week Ford stepping stones are 100yd upstream.

Tucked away under a steep bank among some trees not far from the O Brook are the ruins of two quite well-preserved blowing (or smelting) mills. These were in use in medieval times to extract tin from locally dug ore. They are worth seeing for the mortar and mould stones lying around. Waterwheels supplied the power for the various processes.

From the north side of the stepping stones walk up the lane which gradually bears round to the right. Pass out through a gate, go past a shed and silage pit, and into a field through a waymarked gate. Now make for the top right-hand corner of this field. A signpost stands on the skyline indicating the way, but it is used as a rubbing post and can be pushed over. Exit from the field through a gate in a dip with converging cattle tracks leading to it, and walk down the lane for 200yd to a stile admitting one to a narrower lane. 50yd further on a gate to the left allows you to enter the top corner of the field you entered from the service station at the beginning of the walk.

Make for the far bottom corner and the car park is reached in a few minutes by recrossing the river bridge.

Walk 19

The Abbots' Way and Huntingdon Warren

6 miles (9.5km)

OS sheet 202

An open moor walk, apart from a mile at the beginning and end, this should not be attempted in mist unless you are accomplished with map and compass. The enjoyment of the walk will be greatly enhanced if you take with you a copy of the Dartmoor National Park booklet *The Archaeology of Dartmoor*. The air photograph on page 13 shows in great detail a part of the moor covered in this walk.

The walk begins at Cross Furzes, a signposted crossroads 2½ miles up a long lane from Buckfastleigh. From Buckfastleigh turn up Wallaford Road. Park your car on the open space by the signpost.

Walk down the rough track from the road (signposted as a right of way) to the two-span clapper bridge over the Dean Burn. This is one of the best of these bridges on the moor because of its situation and completeness, and the fact that various initials and dates are inscribed thereon. The date 1737 is easily deciphered. There is a path junction. Take the right fork.

Now pass through the gate and take the path up and across Lambs Down following a line of marker posts. Ignore a well-worn track which pursues a course lower down the hillside. Your immediate destination is Water Oke Corner, a cluster of scrappy, storm-shattered trees in a triangular enclosure where the fields meet the moor, but the path bends round a small stream to save a steep climb.

This is the line of the so-called Abbots' Way. Some Dartmoor writers have suggested it was a cross-Dartmoor route between Buckfast Abbey on the eastern border of the moor, and the two abbeys of Buckland and Tavistock on the west. But the name is first found as late as 1790, so the proposition may be without foundation. The route is somewhat incomplete; here it certainly exists, but once on the open moor it fades away for ½ mile or so.

Go through the gate on to the open moor and look back at the view. Widecombe church tower can be seen in the cleavage of the East Webburn valley and Teignmouth stands at the outfall of its estuary, with the sea beyond. Now walk uphill parallel with the wall on your left, keeping straight on when the corner is passed. As indicated in the previous paragraph, this section is trackless, but the direction is slightly south of west, and if the day is clear 200yd after the wall is left behind the summit cairn of Eastern Whittabarrow is

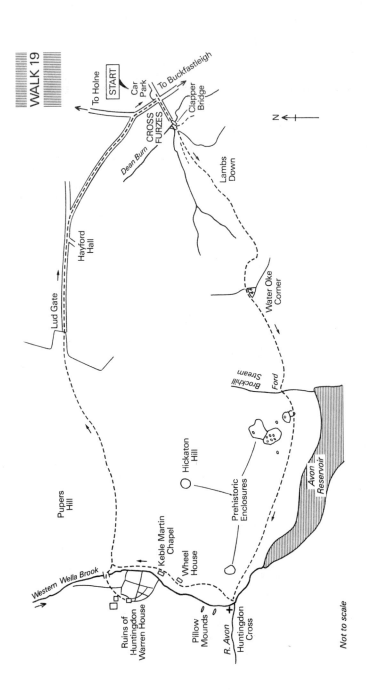

To Holne

START

Car Park

To Buckfastleigh

Clapper Bridge

CROSS FURZES

Dean Burn

Lambs Down

N

Lud Gate

Hayford Hall

Water Oke Corner

Brockhill Stream

Ford

Pupers Hill

Hickaton Hill

Prehistoric Enclosures

Avon Reservoir

Western Wella Brook

Keble Martin Chapel

Wheel House

Ruins of Huntingdon Warren House

Pillow Mounds

R. Avon

Huntingdon Cross

Not to scale

seen 1½ miles away looking rather like a nuclear submarine stranded ark-like on the Ararat which is Brent Moor! Aim for the cairn, and when going down the other side of this easily graded hill the Avon reservoir comes into view, and the point to make for now is the ford in the side-valley ahead.

Cross this stream – the Brockhill Stream – at Brockhill Ford beside the reservoir fencing, and carry on along the obvious track which is once again the (presumed) Abbots' Way. About 300yd beyond the ford a fine collection of Bronze Age huts and enclosures can be seen, right, near the track, and are worth deviating slightly to examine.

The reservoir was built between 1954 and 1957 to supply south Devon, and the water surface is 50 acres in extent.

The way is clear for ¾ mile beyond the prehistoric remains, when a side-stream comes in from the north. This is the Western Wella Brook. Here the reservoir fencing ends and is carried across the Avon by an ugly water gate. Beyond the side-stream is Huntingdon Cross, a simple monument of unknown age. These isolated crosses don't mark graves, but were probably erected in an age of piety to mark a route.

Do not cross the Western Wella Brook, but make your way up the east (left) bank of the brook, picking your way between the wet patches of ground. If you have got with you the booklet mentioned at the beginning of this walk you are now progressing from left to right across the middle of the air photograph on page 13. You thread your way among the waste tips of the medieval tin streamers. On the hillside across the brook are many pillow mounds aligned down-slope. These were made by the warrener at Huntingdon Warren (upstream) as artificial breeding sites for the rabbits which were bred here for flesh and fur in the last century.

The ruined stone walls ½ mile up the brook shielded a nineteenth-century waterwheel from the wind. The wheel was used to pump a mine some distance away, and the water came from the brook. The leat embankment is 80yd to the north. In a gulley 10yd west of the embankment is a small open-to-the-sky chapel, with seats at the downhill end and an upright stone at the top bearing an incised cross. This little place of worship was built by the Martin brothers in 1909 when they were camped near Huntingdon Cross. Many years later, one of them, Keble Martin, became the best-selling author/il-lustrator of *The Concise British Flora*.

Across the stream are the ruins of Huntingdon Warren house, and upstream the approach track crosses the brook by a primitive bridge of five lengths of stone laid side by side.

Now take the track going east over the shoulder of Pupers Hill, and down to Lud Gate. Another mile brings the walker back to his car at Cross Furzes.

Walk 20   The Avon Valley and Shipley Bridge
5 or 10 miles (8 or 16km)

OS sheet 202

This is a fairly gentle walk, part path, part quiet road. Park your car at the Dartmoor end of the car park on the site of South Brent station and railway goods yard. The station closed in 1964. South Brent is nearly at the southernmost tip of the National Park, and is just off the A38 dual carriageway.

Before setting off on the walk as decribed, have a look around the small town. The church is especially interesting, being different to most Dartmoor churches. The massive Norman tower was once the central tower of a cruciform building, but the western part was demolished, probably in the fourteenth century. Look out for the conspicuous market toll house in the main street, still exhibiting its 1889 scale of tolls, and there are a couple of interesting old pubs. The Anchor Hotel was a staging house for the London coaches.

From the car park turn left onto the railway bridge approach, then at once right down a signposted path beside a house called 'Riverside'. The path goes beneath the railway then follows the river Avon to Lydia Bridge. Look out for many birds along here, particularly the robin, wren, tree creeper and dipper. The latter, a black bird with a white breast, bobs about on the stones in the river and sometimes walks beneath its surface. The path is supposed to be haunted by a monk in a red habit.

Lydia Bridge is approached by time-smoothed steps. On the bridge, turn left and 150yd along, and round the first corner, a signposted stile is seen right. This admits the walker to a narrow path between walls.

It bears left and crosses a stone slab stile into a field. Make for the next stile slightly uphill and ⅔ of the way along the hedge. Continue to the next slab stile visible ahead. Now climb slightly uphill, making for a gap in the next hedge where the woodland peters out. From here make for the roof of a cottage 200yd away where a stile gives access to the road. Turn right and follow this road to Shipley Bridge, taking the right turn at a fork on the way. The large sprawl of buildings you will pass is the disused Didworthy Hospital. At Shipley Bridge is a pleasant open space, and it is from here that the walk can be extended up-river along a tarmac road beside the river. However, you should not be troubled by traffic as it is a Water Authority road.

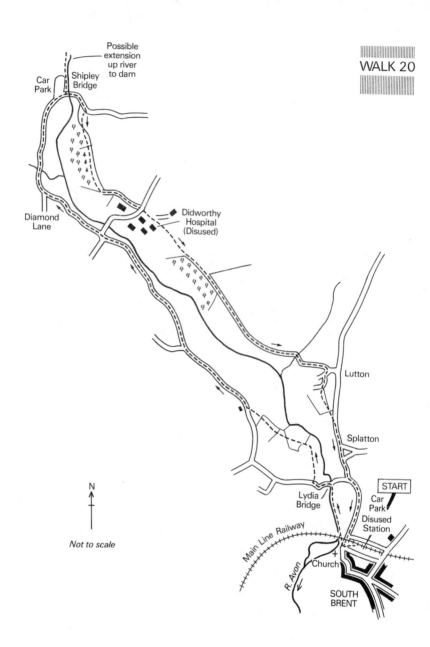

Possible
extension
up river
to dam

Car
Park

Shipley
Bridge

WALK 20

Diamond
Lane

Didworthy
Hospital
(Disused)

Lutton

Splatton

N

Not to scale

START
Car
Park

Disused
Station

Lydia
Bridge

Main Line Railway

R. Avon

Church

SOUTH
BRENT

The road leads directly to the dam of the Avon reservoir (1954–7) and passes through fine river valley scenery on the way. So long as you stay on the road no further directions need be given. The extra distance is five miles there and back, but of course you can shorten the extra distance at any stage by returning when you wish.

There are several features to look out for. The Hunters' Stone, 300yd up-river from the bridge, is a large block of stone beside the road bearing the incised names of celebrated huntsmen of the past. Then, as one passes through a narrow part of the valley somewhat overgrown with rhododendrons, a small memorial to a little girl who was drowned in the river in 1863 will be seen on a rock to your left. Immediately past this are the ruins of Brent Moor House, originally a private house, latterly a Youth Hostel, and finally demolished in 1968 after being empty for some time.

The massive stone walls at Shipley Bridge were built in connection with the china clay workings at Redlake, miles away in the middle of southern Dartmoor. The clay was brought here on a wooden-railed tramway for processing.

Now cross the bridge to the east side and walk 200yd to just past the cattle grid, and enter a signposted and waymarked path. Initially it climbs, then levels out and follows the top edge of woodland. Just before the disused hospital it drops steeply down a rough lane to meet a road in the midst of the complex, and there is a signpost here.

Carry straight on, climbing up through an impressive grove of stately beeches. The way is clear from here, and follows a mixture of field edges and ancient lanes with fine views across the valley. Just before Lutton is reached the path drops steeply to a ford with a single span clapper bridge beside it, then climbs steeply to Lutton Green. At the letterbox turn right, bear left before a large house and enter a gate facing you. By keeping the hedge to your left you will now be led via a couple of stiles to the Brent road. Turn right and South Brent is reached in ¾ mile.

Walk 21   Harford and the Erme Valley

4½ miles (7km)

OS sheet 202

This is a gentle walk, but there is a likelihood of mud after rain. Park your car on the approach to the disused station at Ivybridge, which is a small town at the southern extremity of the National Park. Drive up the west side of the Erme from the town, under the railway viaduct and turn sharp left just beyond.

From the station approach walk towards the river Erme, and notice the old piers (uprights) of the bridge which were part of Brunel's original viaduct and pre-dated the present structure. The old piers bore a timber superstructure.

Take the signposted track heading uphill through the woods. This is the approach drive to Pithill farm which the route bypasses, bearing left when within 100yd of the farm. However, where the lane turns left by a large shed enter the right-hand gate and keep the hedge on your left. There are now superb views ahead of southern Dartmoor with the Erme valley in the middle distance.

When the path reaches the isolated farm of Wilkeys Moor use the ladder stiles provided to circumvent the farmyard. The path then continues beyond the farm along an ancient lane, which bears left and ends at a field gate. Follow the bottom hedge, then cross a field to a hunting gate and enter scrubland. The path is now clear to the next hunting gate where a wood is entered. Take the left path 10yd inside the gate; the right path is marked private. Leave the wood and enter a field, turning right and making for a gate in the north corner. Now go straight across the field to a wall corner from where a straight lane leading to the road at Hall farm is used.

At the road turn right and follow it to the tiny village of Harford. The church is worth visiting. It has a good ceiling and a brass in the chancel. Notice also a curious round-headed memorial to John Prideaux and his wife made of painted copper.

Leave the rook-clattering churchyard by the lichgate and 15yd up the lane enter Butterbrook drive. About 100yd along here enter a gate left and follow the field edge down to a clapper bridge with a hunting gate. Now climb the rocky field on a well-marked path to an iron kissing gate. Pass through here and head for the top of the field when the next iron gate is visible ahead. Make for the gate then follow the hedge to a large stone slab stile which gives access to a grassy corner and the road 15yd beyond.

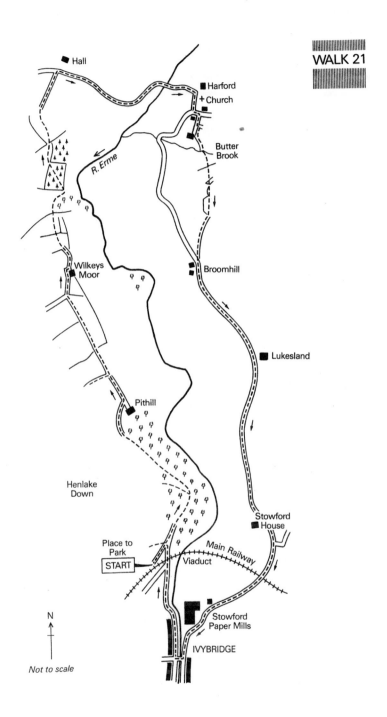

Hall

Harford
+ Church

Butter
Brook

R. Erme

Wilkeys
Moor

Broomhill

Lukesland

Pithill

Henlake
Down

Stowford
House

Place to
Park
START

Main Railway

Viaduct

Stowford
Paper Mills

IVYBRIDGE

N

Not to scale

WALK 21

The road is now followed back to Ivybridge. The fine stone house, Lukesland, was used as Baskerville Hall by a film crew producing *The Hound of the Baskervilles* some years ago.

Just beyond the railway bridge a stone will be seen at the roadside inscribed 'Two Moors Way 29 May 1976'. This commemorates the opening of this long-distance footpath from Ivybridge across Dartmoor, mid-Devon and Exmoor to Lynton on the North Devon coast. A guidebook describes its route.

As the path drops steeply down into Ivybridge the Stowford Paper Mills of Wiggins Teape are passed, and you cross the Erme by the original Ivy Bridge, still with some ivy growing upon it. Turn right and a short walk brings you back to the car.

Walk 22   Trowlesworthy and the Plym Valley

2 miles (3km)

OS sheet 202

This is a gentle walk suitable for young and old, but take care in bad weather. The start of this walk is 700yd east of Cadover Bridge, where the river Plym leaves the open moor, and standing on the minor road cutting across the south-west corner of the National Park between Ivybridge and Yelverton. Park your car where a track leaves the road and heads for Trowlesworthy farm.

The eye-catching features hereabouts are the white spoil tips of the china clay workings. The kaolinization of granite, its chemical decomposition, produces this white substance which is in so much demand for crockery, and as an inert filler for cosmetics, paper, rubber, plastics and paint. Some of the waste is used to make building blocks and bricks, but the rest is piled up beside the pits. The workings began in the 1830s.

Walk along the rough track away from the road, and cross the bridge over the Blacka Brook. Here you enter the National Trust property.

As the track rises notice the humps and bumps across the river. These are the tailings of old stream tin workings. The gravels and stones of the valley bottom were worked over for tin-bearing rocks. The area is known as Brisworthy Burrows.

After a small cutting, where the track bears right, continue straight ahead towards a wall corner. Beside the corner is a rabbit bury, an artificially-prepared rabbit burrow. Trowlesworthy was one of many warrens in the Plym valley, providing meat throughout the year before the days of refrigeration, with the skins as a by-product. Trowlesworthy was the last warren to carry on this trade on Dartmoor, having begun about 1300. It became legally impossible to breed wild rabbits in the 1950s when the opportunity was taken of the myxomatosis epidemic to attempt to eradicate the rabbit altogether.

Contour along, and at the far end of an enclosure to the left, cross an old wall and bear up right passing ancient enclosures. Now make for Shadyback Tor, 150yd ahead. This is a fairly small rockpile, un-named on the Ordnance Survey maps.

Look across the Plym from here. Legis Tor is opposite, and the Legis Lake (perversely, a lake is a small stream on Dartmoor!) flows into the Plym below where we are standing. Its course has been

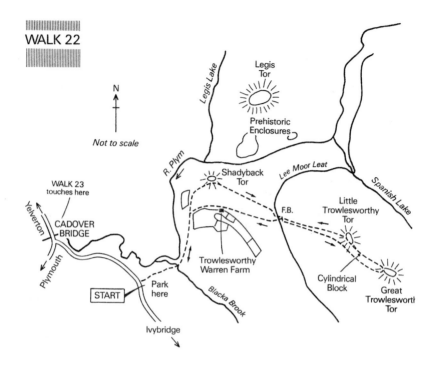

much turned over by the medieval tin streamers. Between Legis Tor and the river are the tell-tale ruined walls of Bronze Age enclosures.

Now turn away and head uphill on a line with Little Trowlesworthy Tor, walking on the top of an old bank. At the Lee Moor leat, which provides water from the Plym for the clay works, turn right and cross the leat by a wide bridge.

Head straight for the nearest rocks of the tor, 900yd ahead, looking out for some fine Bronze Age huts halfway up the slope. At the tor you will see a small quarry on its north side, and much squared and cut stone lying about. The stone of Trowlesworthy, being red granite, was much in demand for ornamental purposes. Between Little Trowlesworthy Tor and Great Trowlesworthy Tor, 400yd beyond, is a conspicuous discarded stunted stone cylinder which was cut in 1823 with the intention of using it as a flagpole base in connection with Devonport's independence celebrations, but for some reason it was never used.

To return, make for the right side of Trowlesworthy farm. There is a rabbit bury near the wall as you approach the house and another beyond the last farm building. You will also notice huts and ancient enclosures. Surely it is a miracle they have survived so long and have not been plundered for subsequent building purposes? The track is to your left now, and will take you back to the starting point of the walk.

Walk 23

4 miles (6.5km)

The Dewerstone and the Middle Reach of the River Plym

OS sheets 201 and 202

There is a not-too-steep climb at the start of this varied walk; it is then fairly level. Walk 22 could be grafted on to the route at the halfway point.

Leave your car in the car park at Shaugh Bridge, which is at the meeting point of the rivers Meavy and Plym, two miles east of the main A386 where it crosses Roborough Down just north of Plymouth.

To get your bearings, first of all stand on Shaugh Bridge itself. This is sited just downstream from the confluence of the rivers Meavy (left) and Plym (right). The present bridge dates from the 1820s and replaced a bridge severely damaged by flood in January 1823. On that occasion the moor had been covered with snow, but a sudden thaw, combined with heavy rain, caused the rivers to rise with catastrophic effect.

Now cross the footbridge to the National Trust property between the two rivers, and take the wide path rising on the river Plym side of the promontory. The path is rough and rocky and doesn't follow either river, but climbs steadily and straight to a sharp bend to the left. Here it levels out and passes a small quarry, then bends to the right passing between a 15ft rock pinnacle and a large block of rock. In fact, it was cut through the granite.

It is obvious from the carefully graded track that we are on the line of a railway system constructed to extract stone from the various quarries on the hillside. The path descends slightly, then a straight uphill section is seen ahead. Go up here, and notice the stone sleepers still *in situ*. The rails have gone.

This was an inclined plane. Two parallel tracks operated simultaneously; the full trucks descending pulled the empty trucks up, rather like a cliff railway. At the top are the remains of the cable drum house, with the spindle still visible. Just below the top, notice how generations of badgers have excavated heaps of earth across the inclined plane.

Now take the higher path gently upwards, passing small quarries with tips opposite and rejected squared stones scattered about. Where the railway track clearly ended continue uphill and the summit rocks are reached just beyond the tree line. This is the top of the Dewerstone, and various inscriptions can be seen cut in the

75

WALK 23

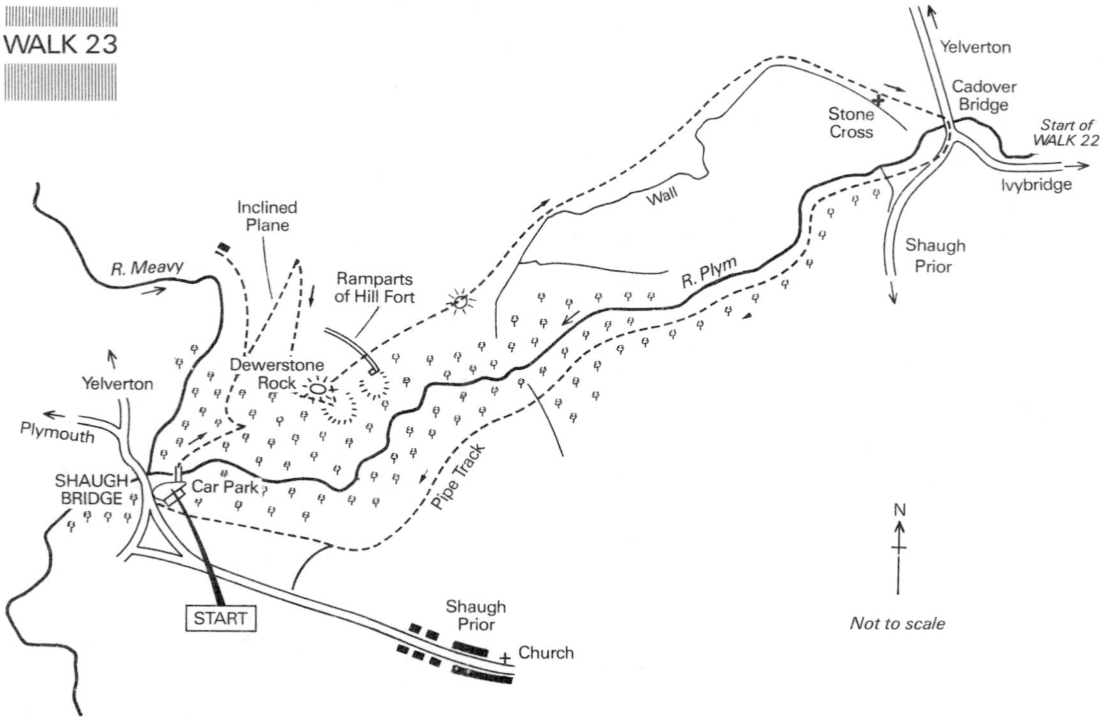

Not to scale

N

Yelverton

Cadover Bridge

Start of WALK 22

Ivybridge

Stone Cross

Shaugh Prior

Wall

R. Plym

Pipe Track

Shaugh Prior

Church

Ramparts of Hill Fort

Inclined Plane

Dewerstone Rock

Car Park

START

R. Meavy

Yelverton

SHAUGH BRIDGE

Plymouth

rocks, notably the one to N.T.Carrington, who published a lengthy poem about Dartmoor in 1826. At one time it was suggested that a memorial might be raised to him up here, to be executed by the architect John Wightwick, but the scheme came to nothing. Instead one finds the words 'Carrington – Obiit Septembris MDCCCXXX' incised in the rock. Carrington is buried at Combe Hay near Bath.

Now take in the view. Plymouth Breakwater is plainly seen, and near at hand Bickleigh Camp (Royal Marines). Our return route is visible contouring the hillside to the south.

Before setting off across the open moor, go down about 80yd along a green path to get a top view of the main rock climbing faces which are on the Plym side of this great thrusting spur. They will be seen again from across the valley. The Dewerstone gives the best rock climbing on Dartmoor. In 1960 a climber found a late Bronze Age (1000 BC) drinking cup in a rock crevice. It is now in Plymouth Museum.

Return to the summit and head north-east making for some prominent un-named rocks in line with the top edge of the woods beyond. As you leave the Dewerstone spur you will pass through the ruins of two dry-stone walls. These were defensive ramparts thrown up by Iron Age people when the summit was used as a promontory fort. In the same way many coastal headlands were developed as refuges in times of inter-tribal warfare.

After passing the cluster of rocks the route to follow is along the outside of the enclosure walls, and after a mile this will bring you down to Cadover Bridge past a stone cross standing in a socket stone which is itself sited within a circular earthwork. The modern shaft is of red granite, presumably from Trowlesworthy Tor (see Walk 22). This cross was discovered by troops exercising here in 1873 and set up by them. The shaft is a more recent restoration. From here the china clay works are much in evidence (see Walk 22 for details).

Cross the road bridge, turn right and follow the river bank. On reaching the fence climb the signposted stile which is about 20yd from the river. The path follows a broken pipeline and is waymarked where route-finding might be difficult. The pipe carried china clay in suspension to the Shaugh Bridge drying works and as a result this is called the Pipe Track.

The further you walk along this path, the more the crags of the Dewerstone become visible opposite, perhaps with climbers clinging to them. When the path meets a dirt road this is used for a short distance, but should then be left and the signposted and waymarked path followed steeply downhill to the car park.

Walk 24   Burrator Reservoir
4 miles (6.5km)

OS sheet 202

This is a simple level walk which is suitable for parents with a pushchair as it follows the public tarmac road round the reservoir. Two short diversions can be added, and these are included in the distance given above. It is probably not very enjoyable on a day when a lot of cars are on the move.

Burrator reservoir is reached by turning off the B3212 at Dousland, 1½ miles from Yelverton. Park near the dam.

The reservoir was formed in 1898 to solve the water storage problems of the expanding city of Plymouth. The dam was heightened in 1928 to increase the capacity, and while this was being done traffic reached Sheepstor by a suspension bridge strung across the arm of the reservoir beside the dam.

Leave the area of the dam and walk along the western side of the reservoir keeping right at the fork just beyond Burrator Lodge. The pre-reservoir approach to Sheepstor was down a lane opposite the north gate of the Lodge.

From the tail of the reservoir there is a fine view up left to Leather Tor, which has been likened to the Matterhorn as seen from Zermatt. Certainly it is one of the most dramatic of Dartmoor's 200 or so tors – from this angle.

At the end of the reservoir continue around, ignoring tracks off to the left, and follow the road along the east side. About ⅔ mile along here pay a visit to the very interesting Longstone peninsula, which juts out into the reservoir.

Climb the stile beside the iron gate and look at the forlorn ruins of Longstone Manor. Nearby are a variety of stone remains. Four or five stone troughs, a crusher and edge runner. At the water's edge beyond the ruin is another trough. About 50yd from the ruin, but invisible from it because of the trees, is a windstrew or winnowing platform. Here the threshing was done, allowing the breezes to carry off the chaff. Now walk round the promontory, taking care not to disturb any anglers or the fish. The shoreline path will bring you back to the starting point as the peninsula is almost an island.

Back on the road, resume your circumnavigation of the reservoir, but at the next T-junction turn left to view the tiny village and church of Sheepstor which takes its name from the tor which looms up behind. Seek out the elaborate tomb of the Brooke family in the

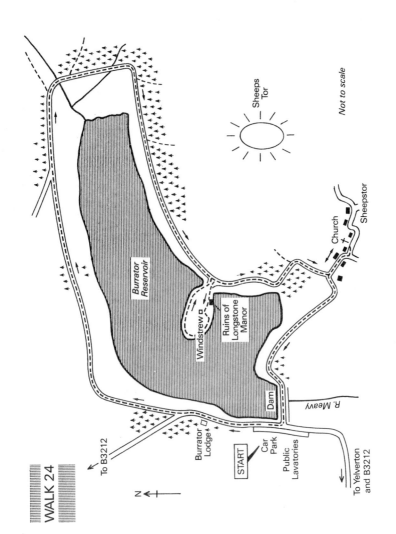

WALK 24

Not to scale

Sheeps Tor

Sheepstor

Church

Burrator Reservoir

Windstrew □

Ruins of Longstone Manor

R. Meavy

Dam

To B3212

Burrator Lodge

START

Car Park

Public Lavatories

To Yelverton and B3212

N

churchyard. These were the famous white rajahs of Sarawak, uncle and nephew, who ruled that far eastern country during the last century. Sir John Brooke died at Burrator House, near the dam, in 1868. Later it was occupied by C.E.Brittan (1870–1949), probably the most accomplished Dartmoor painter.

Bull-baiting was formerly carried out in the vicarage field near the church. A bull was secured to a well-anchored rock and then baited, or tormented, by dogs. At these barbarous festivities the women wore special aprons in which they caught the bull-dog when it was thrown. It was the custom to bury the dogs which were killed on the spot.

Now retrace your steps to the T-junction, and take the road heading down past the Old School House. The dam and car park are reached in about ⅓ mile.

Walk 25

6 miles (9.5km)

The Walkham Valley and the Merrivale Antiquities

OS sheet 191

This is a varied walk on tracks or open moor, with very little climbing. There is trackless moor at the end, so take care in mist.

Park your car by the old bridge over the river Walkham near the Dartmoor Inn at Merrivale on the B3357 between Tavistock and Two Bridges.

Climb up the embankment to the 'new' road, cross it, and enter the signposted farm track beside Hillside Cottages. The heaps of worked stone inside the gate were dumped here when the Napoleonic War warders' quarters in Princetown were demolished in the 1960s.

A quarry is passed, then Long Ash farm, no longer used as such. On the lower side of the yard are the remains of the old farmstead. Across the valley is Vixen Tor, a magnificent pile, perhaps seen at its best from here. It can be climbed, but is quite a scramble. Do not attempt it from here, as the permitted approach is from the far side.

Carry on along the track and cross the Long Ash Brook (sometimes called the Pila Brook).Where the track leaves the woods head uphill for 50yd or so, and you will find the low ruined walls of Hucken farm. The most distinctive feature is the set of twelve upright stones of the rickyard. They served to keep the ricks off the ground and away from rats and damp, and allowed air to circulate. Also here are the remains of the farmhouse and outbuildings.

Return now to the track and follow it along to Hucken Tor, a charming feature, much grown over with foliage. A gate is actually built between the rocks of the tor and passing through a fine view opens up ahead.

The track is now straightforward and generally downhill for over one mile. Three farms are passed: Parktown (right) and Davytown and Withill (left). At the first crossroads turn up left, signposted to Criptor, and after crossing a cattle grid take a track heading off right towards Ingra Tor. Where this track bears right, keep straight on and the line of the disused Princetown branch railway is reached just before the tor.

Turn left along the track, east, and where it passes the mouth of a quarry digress briefly to look inside. It is quite deep. This railway began life as a horse-drawn tramway in the 1820s, was later converted to a conventional railway and closed in 1956. For the last twenty years of its life there was a stopping place here called Ingra

Tor Halt which exhibited a sign reading:

Great Western Railway Company
NOTICE
In the interests of game preservation and
for their own protection against snakes,
dogs should be kept on a lead.
By order

The line continues round the small valley called Yes Tor Bottom. Notice how the original tramway followed a longer route. Being a tramway it could follow curves of a tighter radius. Other examples of this route variation will be seen further on. The ruins of Yes Tor farm on the lower side of the track are passed, and it is worth noting that to cope with the gradient the railway had to travel 2½ miles before doubling back to a point just 400yd uphill from here.

The line straightens out somewhat, and the remains of the Royal Oak Siding, which led to Swell Tor quarry, are seen to the right. Then the line starts its compass-boxing bend and the course of the old tramway is very noticeable.

Stay on the track until the yellow front of Yellowmead farm comes into view on the lower slopes of North Hessary Tor. Now cut down left and head north-east to a wall corner. Follow the wall to a stream, the headwaters of the Long Ash Brook crossed earlier. At the stream head for a tall stone breaking the skyline ahead. (Ignore a larger stone away to your left; this is a prehistoric menhir).

When you have reached the stone you are heading for, notice that it bears two letters, a T and an A. These stand for Tavistock and Ashburton and are clues to the purpose of the stone. It was one of a number erected as guidestones for travellers across this stretch of moor, and probably dates from about 1700.

Now aim for Merrivale quarry on the slopes of Staple Tor. Your course will take you to the Bronze Age remains usually known as the Merrivale antiquities, 200yd from the T/A stone.

Two stone rows (see introduction for a general account of Dartmoor antiquities) run parallel to each other and should be visited first. Walk along the southernmost row. A few yards to your left you will see the despoiled capstone of a kistvaen. The chest itself is undamaged, but someone cut a gatepost or mantlepiece out of the lid. Back at the row a burial site marks the halfway point, and just beyond, another burial mound away from the row seems to be the northern terminal of a third stone row which runs tangentially south-west, and in the general direction of the stone circle and menhir. In this area are examples of nearly all the prehistoric antiquity types to be found on Dartmoor. Advocates of the new branch of archaeology – astro-archaeology – have much to say about Merrivale.

Now head due north towards the road, and a cluster of Bronze

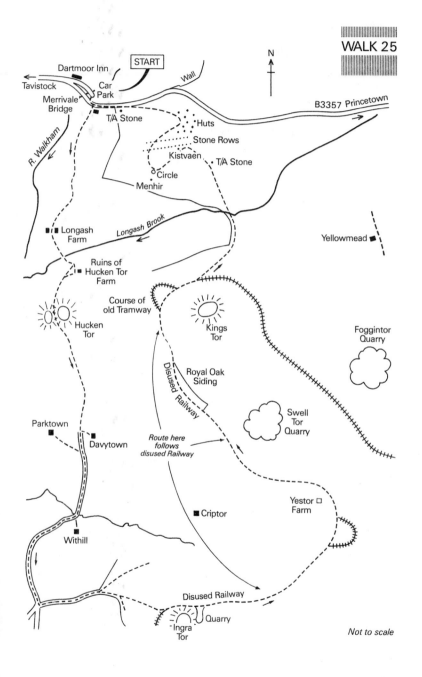

WALK 25

N

START

Dartmoor Inn

Tavistock

Car Park

Merrivale Bridge

T/A Stone

R. Walkham

Wall

B3357 Princetown

Huts

Stone Rows

Kistvaen

T/A Stone

Circle

Menhir

Longash Brook

Longash Farm

Yellowmead

Ruins of Hucken Tor Farm

Course of old Tramway

Hucken Tor

Kings Tor

Foggintor Quarry

Disused Railway

Royal Oak Siding

Swell Tor Quarry

Parktown

Davytown

Route here follows disused Railway

Criptor

Yestor Farm

Withill

Disused Railway

Ingra Tor

Quarry

Not to scale

Age huts will be found. The large flat worked stone lying near them owes nothing to prehistoric workmanship, but is a discarded edge runner from the nineteenth century, rejected in manufacture.

The route back is downhill beside the road to the bridge. On the way you will see another T/A stone 15yd uphill from where the left-hand wall meets the road. Merrivale quarry was begun in 1876, and not having a rail link all stone had to be got off Dartmoor by wagons and later by steam traction engines.

Walk 26   Horrabridge to Sampford Spiney

5 miles (8km)

OS sheet 201

The outward route of this walk is on paths and tracks, the return is mostly on quiet roads. There is one steep climb.

Leave your car in a quiet side road in Horrabridge. The main thoroughfares in Horrabridge are narrow and busy, so avoid causing an obstruction. The village is just off the A386 Yelverton to Tavistock road.

Horrabridge has greatly expanded in recent years, but its centre is attractive and is designated a conservation area. The name puzzles everyone who visits it, and numerous derivations have been suggested. The bridge stands on the boundary between the parishes of Buckland Monachorum and Whitchurch and includes a stone in its structure bearing an incised Latin cross, the actual boundary stone. An old word for boundary is 'har', so 'boundary bridge' has the merit of logicality.

Leave the village by taking the signposted path which goes up from the car park of the Leaping Salmon Inn. It starts as a narrow lane, but soon enters a field, at the top of which there is a stile. Keep the hedge on your left, and pass through a gap into a field containing some large oak trees. Stay by the hedge, leave the field through a gate and turn right along a track which leads to a road.

Go up the road for 10yd, then right over a stile. Follow the well marked tractor tracks across the field. Walkhampton church shows up well across the valley, detached by ½ mile from its village, but serving an enormous parish extending up to the neighbourhood of Princetown.

Turn left by a stone barn, through a gate and right at once. After passing Monkswell House enter the right gate of two, keep the hedge on your left then go along a grassy lane. You pass Monkswell farm and stay on a track which hugs the hedge at the top of two fields. Descend to the road, turn right and after 20yd enter the farmyard of Whimington, left. Go to the left of the house and round the back. Enter an ancient lane which gives way to the top of a steep field. Keep the hedge on your left, descend, cross a stream and step stile. Climb a short distance, then follow an old cart track. Leave the field by a gate at Watery Ford, cross the road and enter a field through a green gate next to a service reservoir.

Now keep the hedge on your right, go through a hunting gate and

85

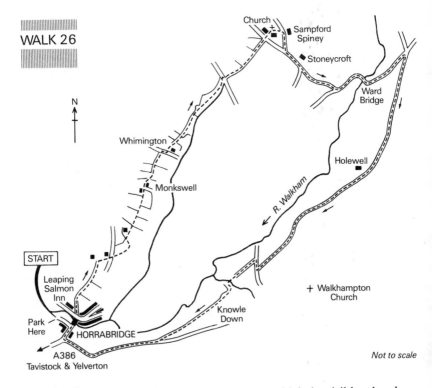

N

Church
Sampford
Spiney

Stoneycroft

Ward
Bridge

Whimington

Holewell

Monkswell

R. Walkham

START

Leaping
Salmon
Inn

+ Walkhampton
Church

Knowle
Down

Park
Here

HORRABRIDGE

A386
Tavistock & Yelverton

Not to scale

make for Sampford Spiney church tower which is visible ahead.
Leave the field by a gate at the foot of the village green, but before
doing so look out for a fine length of wall just before the gate is
reached.

Sampford Spiney is a very atmospheric place; it is hardly a
village. Sampford Manor is a well-built house in the vernacular
tradition, and on the green is the old school and a tall slender cross.
Once it stood in the hedge nearby, but a nineteenth-century Lord of
the Manor had it erected in its present more exalted position.

The church has a typical west-Dartmoor-type tower with large
crocketed pinnacles. On the north side of the church is a forbidding
stone mausoleum belonging to the Godden family. Peer through the
grill in the door, I dare you!

Leave the churchyard by the south-east gate (one can always
work out points of the compass by looking at the orientation of a
church; the altar is at the east end) and go along this quiet road
towards an impressive beech avenue.

Just past a large house called Stoneycroft turn left down an
unmade road which comes out on a tarmac road by a cattle grid.
Continue downhill and cross the river Walkham at Ward Bridge.

The present bridge replaced an older one which was swept away in a flood in July 1890.

Now climb steeply to the crossroads where you must turn right (signposted to Walkhampton) and follow this quiet road for 1½ miles to a T-junction. Turn right here (signposted to Sampford Spiney) for 100yd then left along a lane. Near the bottom it can be wet after rain, and there are stepping stones over a small stream. The track now veers left round some trees and follows the bottom boundary of this patch of open land, Knowle Down, to the road near the outskirts of Horrabridge, from where a walk of ¼ mile brings you back to the centre of the village.

Walk 27

4 miles (6.5km)

Lower Walkham Valley and Double Waters

OS sheet 201

After an initial climb through woodland, this walk is thereafter not strenuous. The route is entirely on tracks and paths.

Leave your car at Grenofen Bridge, which is reached by turning west off the A386 Tavistock–Yelverton road at the Halfway House Inn. After making the turn, take the first left down a steep lane. Park among the trees on the south side of the bridge.

From the car park walk up the steep winding track through the woods. This is obviously an old road, deep cut as it is and leading to an ancient crossing place. It was in fact the original road between Buckland Monachorum and Tavistock, both of which had abbeys in pre-dissolution days. The wood is called Sticklepath Wood; 'stickle' means steep, which is very apt.

When the path leaves the woods it levels out with branches to left and right. These should be ignored as the correct route is straight ahead along a grassy track much used by riders, with tall gorse bushes on both sides and thorn trees scattered about. This is the northern tip of Roborough Down which extends five miles south to the outskirts of Plymouth, but it isn't much visited round here.

When you reach a space at the end used as a car park, turn right down a rubble track marked 'No vehicles beyond this point, except those holding common rights.' A splendid view faces you. The open land opposite is West Down. Depending on the time of year you are visiting the area you may see that bracken is cut for cattle bedding on both sides of the track.

The roughly tarred road ends at the entrance to Bucktor, but continue along the track. Notice water flowing out of an old mine adit left, and observe the many fallen trees. These woods were greatly damaged by the winter storms of early 1978 and 1979. You will see a footbridge over the Walkham, but don't cross it now. Carry on along the track which bears round to the left.

You are now at Double Waters, the meeting place of the rivers Walkham and Tavy, which despite its singular beauty is outside the Dartmoor National Park. Indeed the whole of this walk is just outside the Park boundary which runs north to south across Grenofen Bridge. The first leg of the walk up to the 'No vehicles . . .' sign was along the Park's western boundary. This is so obviously anachronistic that there are moves afoot (June 1979) to extend the

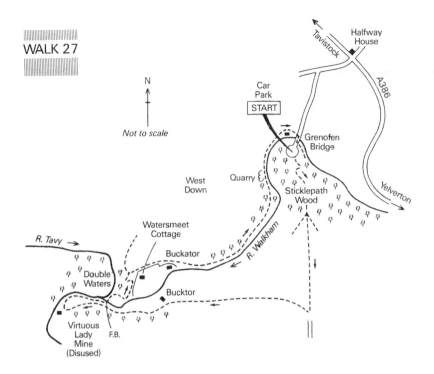

N

Not to scale

Car Park
START

Tavistock

Halfway House

A386

Grenofen Bridge

Quarry

West Down

Sticklepath Wood

Yelverton

R. Tavy →

Watersmeet Cottage

R. Walkham

Buckator

Double Waters

Bucktor

Virtuous Lady Mine (Disused)

F.B.

Park to include Double Waters.

Keep on the track until it begins to climb steadily. Leave it here and walk to the river bank. The house perched on a prominent bluff was the mine captain's house of the Virtuous Lady Mine, and the heaps of rubble lying about among the scattered ruins are connected with the mine (copper). It is thought that the mine is old enough to have been called after Queen Elizabeth I.

Walk back up the river along the bank, cross the footbridge, go round the back of the crag facing you and through the narrow defile on its other side, then up the north bank of the Walkham. The path bends away from the river and climbs past Watersmeet Cottage to a zig-zag. Where a concrete track comes up right, descend along it, past Buckator (note similar spelling to the house opposite; I expect they get their letters muddled) and back down to the Walkham again.

There is now a very pleasant one mile stroll up river with no impediments to straightforward walking. Just past a large crag to the left you will see a mine chimney, and 300yd further on a walled-up-section conceals quarries in the hillside behind. Here the local stone, elvan, was taken out.

As you approach Lower Grenofen House the path conducts you behind the private grounds, then back to the approach drive which leads directly to Grenofen Bridge. Pause on the bridge to see the trout, and possibly salmon, swimming in the deep pool below.

Walk 28

6½ miles (10.5km)

OS sheets 191 or 201

Mary Tavy, Peter Tavy and the Tavy Valley

This is a not-too-strenuous walk, but with a probability of mud at the end. There is plenty of space to leave your car in the road outside Mary Tavy church, which is reached by turning east off the A386 Tavistock–Okehampton road.

Walk down to the footbridge over the river Tavy past the Central Electricity Generating Board power station, the large factory-type building on your right. This is a hydro-electric station whose turbines are run by water brought along converted mine leats. You will follow one of these later in the walk.

Once over the footbridge turn right, and follow the path past the lovely Longtimber Tor (right) to Peter Tavy. Dartmoor tors come in all shapes and sizes and this is one of the most attractive; a mass of trees and rocks. There is a tall crag on the far side of the river.

Peter Tavy church is worth visiting, without having any really special features. Have a look round the village which possesses some pleasant cottages. The Peter Tavy Inn is perhaps the most interesting building in the village, and not only for its structural characteristics!

Now return to the footbridge and take the path which appears to go upstream. After 50yd, by the stile, there are two mining adits on the right, one quite large, and once over the stile you will notice a hefty turbine bed at the foot of a pipe. These remains belong to the Devon United Mine, and tin, copper and arsenic were extracted as recently as 60 years ago. At the top of the pipe, contour left along the upper limit of the mine workings, and pick up a cart track, the old mine road, which will get you out to the road at a tin shed through a couple of gates. On the way you will see more riverside tors lining the far bank of the Tavy.

Turn left and walk along this quiet road for about one mile. You will pass through the pretty hamlet of Cudlipptown, and 500yd beyond look out for a pair of slotted gate posts on your left. Just beyond take the steep rough lane left, but notice the 5ft 6in stone direction post on the corner. 100 years or so ago signposts were made to last.

Cross the Tavy by Horndon Bridge, ascend the hill beyond and turn right at a gate beside the leat. This is one of the two water

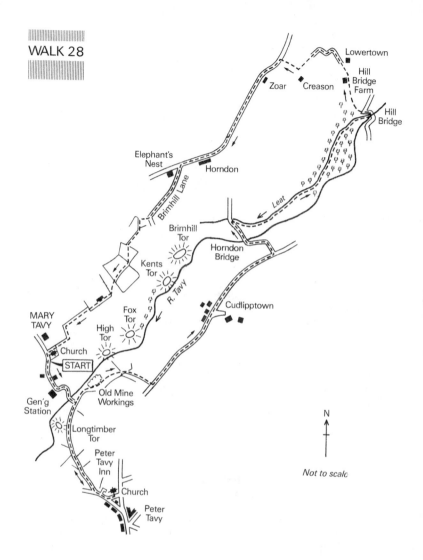

supplies for the power station. The other takes its water from the river in Tavy Cleave, several miles upstream.

You now follow the leat for ¾ mile, walking against the direction of flow. Look out for fish darting away as you approach. In places old tramway lines have been pressed into service as fences or stiles. The engineering skill of the hydraulicians who planned these leats can only be marvelled at when you see the way this one has been blasted out of the hill.

This waterside stroll comes to an end at Hill Bridge, the take-off point of the leat, where you climb to the road up a nine-rung iron ladder. Notice the perforations in the bridge parapets to allow the free flow of flood water.

Turn left uphill, and enter the gate marked Hillbridge farm. The building just inside the gate, now a dwelling, was once a small local school. From here follow the track past the farm, a riding establishment, and Lowertown, a yellow-painted building. Beyond here the route zig-zags and comes out on open land near the entrance to Lower Creason farm. Turn right here, and left at the road.

Now keep on the road past the hamlets of Zoar and Horndon to the pub called the Elephant's Nest. The sharply-pointed hill in the distance is Brent Tor, with a small church on its summit, and even a tiny burial ground.

This area has a very Cornish flavour, due to the cottages being built in the Cornish tradition by the miners who came here to exploit Dartmoor's minerals. Horndon had two places of worship, a Methodist chapel (1904) with a neighbouring Chile pine (monkey puzzle tree); and a barn-like Anglican church (1844) with a bell turret. It hasn't been used since 1960, but can't be sold as the deeds are lost.

Go down Brimhill Lane beside the Elephant's Nest car park. When the lane bears left at the power station header pond climb the stone step stile and make for the nearest wall corner facing you 50yd away. Here is another step stile. Scale it, and turn left along a short lane. Enter a field and follow the right-hand hedge making for a gate. Bear half left here and head for the far corner where there is another step stile. Now follow the hedge facing you to yet another step stile in the corner. Bear half left again and make for the field corner.

Now follow a track, often muddy, past a building with a chimney, and at the bottom of this field you will have a broken wall on your left for company. Where this veers left follow the bottom hedge and turn right at a gate gap. Now follow the hedge to a step stile which admits you to the top east corner of Mary Tavy churchyard.

15yd south of here is the gothic-pointed gravestone, somewhat leaning, of Mr and Mrs William Crossing. William Crossing was a notable Dartmoor authority who died in 1928. His *Guide to Dartmoor*, available as a reprint, is esteemed by some as Holy Writ.

Your car is now a few yards away at the foot of the churchyard.

Walk 29   Doe Tor Brook and Widgery Cross

3 miles (4.8km)

OS sheet 191 or 201

This is a short and easy open-moor walk on north-west Dartmoor. It should not however be attempted in mist unless you are accomplished in map and compass work.

Leave your car just inside the gate at the approach to High Down. This is reached by driving up the rough lane beside the Dartmoor Inn on the A386 Tavistock–Okehampton road, opposite the Lydford turning. Many cars drive over High Down and park near the river Lyd, but this damages the surface of the moor, reduces the grazing and creates a visual shock in the open landscape.

Walk over High Down along the left-hand wall and down to the river Lyd which is crossed by a footbridge or stepping stones. This spot is interesting as being the exact boundary between the granite (east of the river) and the metamorphic rock.

Turn right along a green path which roughly follows the river which falls away on your right. After 200yd look out for a conspicuous rock on the far bank with a couple of seats nearby. A plaque fixed to the rock – Black Rock – serves as a memorial to a young army officer, killed in France in 1918, who had visited the area shortly before his death.

At the point where the Doe Tor Brook hurries beneath the path, turn up left beside the stream and climb steeply past Doe Tor Falls, a modest cataract, keeping on the north bank.

Further up is a fenced area (although the fence is broken and useless) which is meant to keep people and animals out of an area of heaped rubble for safety's sake. This was Foxhole Mine. The actual 'works' were further upstream.

When you reach flattish land at the top of the fast-flowing section you will see a number of red and white poles on your right. These mark the northern boundary of the Willsworthy firing range, and you should on no account pass the line of poles if red flags are flying on high points in the vicinity. However, the route as given does not require you to do so!

Keep on the same bank of the brook and follow it round so that you are heading north, and where the valley begins to narrow you will come across the roofless ruin of the Foxhole Mine building.

This is an interesting site. The house has two chimneys and is better preserved than many similar sites. Perhaps this is because it is

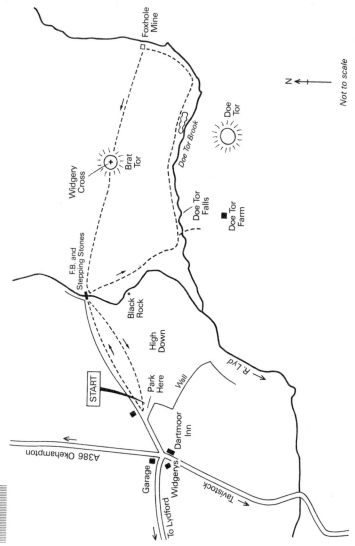

WALK 29

Foxhole Mine

Doe Tor

Widgery Cross

Brat Tor

Doe Tor Brook

Doe Tor Falls

Doe Tor Farm

F.B. and Stepping Stones

Black Rock

High Down

START

Park Here

Wall

R. Lyd

Dartmoor Inn

Garage

Widgerys

To Lydford

A386 Okehampton

Tavistock

Not to scale

N

tucked away and remote from the much-frequented trade routes of potential vandals. They are even present on Dartmoor, I am afraid.

In front of the ruin are the remains of two buddles, circular devices for sorting the tin concentrates after crushing, and to the north is the filled-up wheel pit and tail race with the ramp and leat along which the water was conducted to the wheel.

Now turn your back on the Doe Tor Brook and head westwards to the summit of Brat Tor (sometimes engagingly spelt Bra Tor!) which has a stone cross on its highest point. It is not a single hewn monolith, but an aggregate of built-up blocks constructed to mark Queen Victoria's silver jubilee in 1887 on the instruction of Mr William Widgery, a well-known Dartmoor artist. His house, now called Widgery's, faces you across the A386 as you reach the main road at the end of the rough lane.

William Crossing tells the story of Widgery painting on the moor when an acquaintance passed by, looked over his shoulder and failed to recognise the picture being painted from the view before him. In the foreground instead of a marsh there was a rocky stream. 'Mr Widgery' said the visitor mildly, 'there is no river at the foot of that hill.' 'Isn't there?' returned the artist, without looking up: 'Well, there ought to be'. I sometimes wonder if the passer-by was Crossing himself!

Stop here to take in the view. To the west, if the day is clear, Bodmin Moor forms the skyline. At the foot of the tor the Lyd threads its way, and over to the north-west is the rounded hill known as Great Nodden. Look carefully and you will see the line of the long-disused railway curling round its plum-pudding form. This enterprise carried down peat from extensive beds beyond Great Links Tor, the fine feature to the north-east.One of its optimistic promoters even visualised running the British Navy on peat instead of coal.

Now descend the tor to the footbridge, and return to your car across High Down.

The Meldon Reservoir, West Okement Valley and the Sourton Tors

OS sheet 191

This is an open moor walk with some climbing. It should not be attempted in mist unless you are accomplished in map and compass work.

Leave your car in the public car park at Meldon reservoir. There are public lavatories. This is reached by turning off the A30 at the signposted road junction 2½ miles west of Okehampton. (Some years hence, when the Okehampton bypass is built, this road will be downgraded from its present A30 status.)

From the car park walk to the far end of the dam, and look about you. The reservoir was built between 1970 and 1972 after a protracted argument going back to 1962. Those who knew the valley before cannot agree that the dam has improved the scene. Down the valley is a large quarry where much of the ballast for British Rail originates.

From this end of the dam take the track for 100yd, but instead of entering a gate bear up left past scattered thorn trees. Over a rise, aim for the head of a steep narrow valley entering the reservoir from the south. This is the Fishcombe Water. To accomplish this, pick up a sheep path to facilitate progress across the steep slope. You are climbing diagonally across the hill all the time.

Go past a small cascade which is a delightful sequestered corner. Mountain ash and hollies grow here. Follow the tiny stream up trying to stay on dry ground, with the headwater springs on your right.

Keep looking ahead, and when the twin humps of Black Tor come into view ahead, make towards them, then drop steeply downhill to the West Okement river. As you descend you will be just outside the northern limits of Black Tor Copse, one of the three old, natural oak woods of Dartmoor. The wood is sometimes called Black Tor Beare, which means the same thing; 'Beare' is an old name for a wood.

It is thought that many Dartmoor valleys once had similar groves, but Wistmans Wood beside the West Dart river at Two Bridges and Piles Copse up the Erme from Ivybridge are all that remain. Tin miners, fuel scavengers, grazing animals and fire are thought to be responsible for the depletion. For the sites which have survived we can probably thank the rocky slopes out of which they grow, and they are now protected by various official designations.

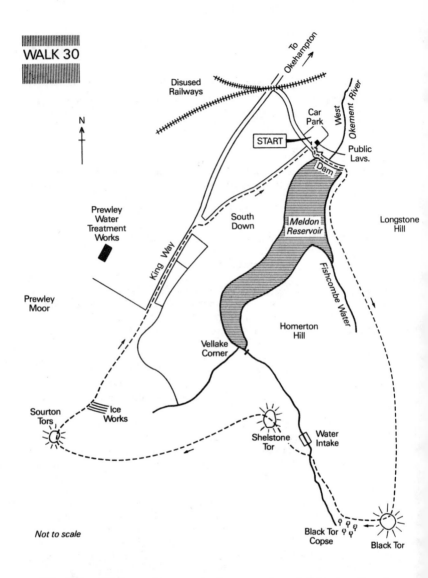

WALK 30

N

Disused
Railways

To Okehampton

West Okement River

Car
Park

START

Public
Lavs.

Dam

Prewley
Water
Treatment
Works

South
Down

*Meldon
Reservoir*

Longstone
Hill

King Way

Prewley
Moor

Fishcombe Water

Homerton
Hill

Vellake
Corner

Sourton
Tors

Ice
Works

Shelstone
Tor

Water
Intake

Not to scale

Black Tor
Copse

Black Tor

The West Okement has now to be crossed, and this can often be
done by stepping from rock to rock just upstream from the walled
water intake 500yd down-river from the north end of the copse. If
the river is running high this should not be attempted. There is a
footbridge ½ mile downstream at Vellake Corner.

Assuming you have crossed near the intake, climb now to
Shelstone Tor, then walk due west across a smooth-turfed bowl to

the crested Sourton Tors, a mile away on the skyline. As you climb the last 300yd to the tors you will cross the line of an ancient track, the King Way, the original route between Okehampton and Tavistock. (The obvious way up from the footbridge links with the Shelstone Tor route here.)

Having feasted on the view, and the Bristol Channel is sometimes visible, head north-east and aim for a long hedge to the right of the prominent Prewley water treatment works. A little distance down from the summit you will come across five or six long, shallow, grass-grown troughs. They look more like earthworks than anything else. They were so constructed that water would fill them so that ice would form. The ice was hurried down to Plymouth for the fishing industry as required. In the gulley below the lowest trough is all that remains of a subterranean ice house, where the ice was stored. This site was chosen as it was elevated, north facing and handy to the railway for rapid transmission to Plymouth. A nearby spring provided the water. Even so, it wasn't one of Dartmoor's more sucessful ventures; most of the ice melted in transit! The site is marked on the 1889 6in map as Ice Ponds, and appears to have been fenced in.

Enter a lane – you are now on the King Way – by a line of prominent hedgerow beeches, and carry on along here until when nearly abreast of the highest part of South Down to the right, a wall faces you. Bear right round the outside of the wall, and don't enter the narrow lane. Keep the hedge on your left and follow it down to the reservoir car park.